GOWER SHIPWRECKS

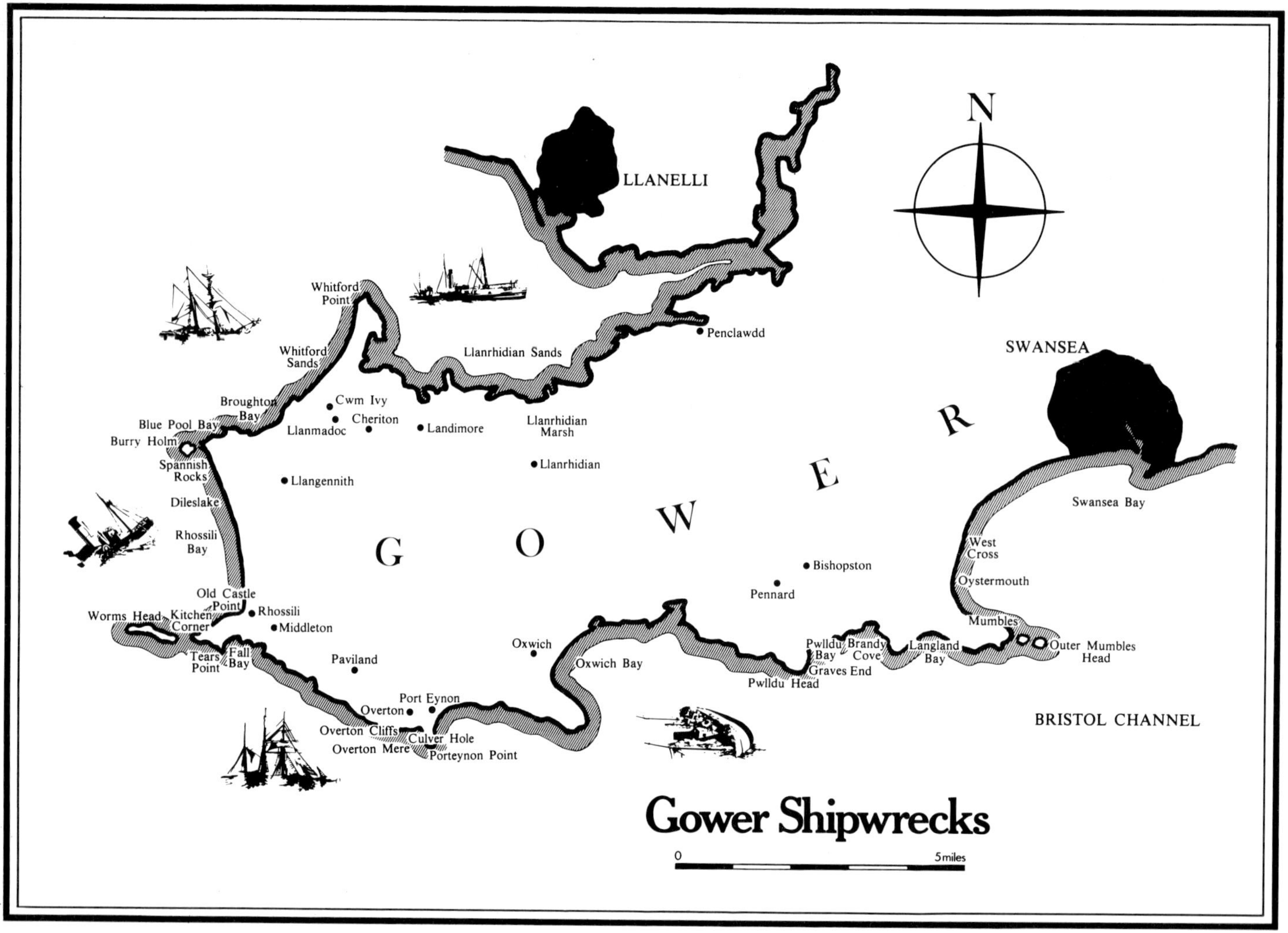
LLANELLI
N
SWANSEA
Whitford Point
Whitford Sands
Llanrhidian Sands
Penclawdd
Broughton Bay
Blue Pool Bay
Burry Holm
Spannish Rocks
Cwm Ivy
Cheriton
Llanmadoc
Landimore
Llanrhidian Marsh
Llanrhidian
Llangennith
Dileslake
Rhossili Bay
G O W E R
Swansea Bay
West Cross
Oystermouth
Bishopston
Pennard
Old Castle Point
Worms Head
Kitchen Corner
Rhossili
Middleton
Tears Point
Fall Bay
Paviland
Oxwich
Oxwich Bay
Mumbles
Pwlldu Bay
Brandy Cove
Langland Bay
Outer Mumbles Head
Graves End
Pwlldu Head
Port Eynon
Overton
Overton Cliffs
Culver Hole
Overton Mere
Porteynon Point
BRISTOL CHANNEL
Gower Shipwrecks
0
5 miles

GOWER SHIPWRECKS

P. H. REES

CHRISTOPHER DAVIES

First Published by
Christopher Davies (Publishers) Ltd.,
P.O. Box 403, Sketty,
Swansea, SA2 9BE.

Reprinted 1988

ISBN 0 7154 0705 8

*Set in 12 on 14 Baskerville and
Printed in Wales by
Dynevor Printing Company,
Rawlings Road, Llandybïe, Dyfed.*

To my wife Maria

Foreword

During the summer months, the Gower Penninsula offers the visitor a wealth of natural beauty, long golden beaches, cloudless skies and blue waters. During the winter, however, Gower takes on a somewhat different character, one which offers far greater excitement and beauty. Deserted beaches, the winds tearing the hedgerows, grey Atlantic breakers pounding the beaches, all take me back to those days when Gower was void of caravans, multi-coloured tents, crowded car parks and plastic paraphernalia. Walking along these winter swept beaches and cliffs first took my imagination back to those days of sail, when the South Westerly gales hammered against the shores driving many a vessel hard upon the rocks and the sand bars. The number of vessels lost in Gower waters is considerable. This book does not attempt to examine them all; it simply gives an account of the more interesting and well known wrecks, and some of the less well known about which accurate records exist.

To the organisations and institutions who gave me valuable assistance in my researches I express my gratitude, as I do to members of their staffs for their patience and readiness with advice. The helpfulness of the Swansea Public Library and the Gower Society was especially valuable.

Peter H. Rees

Acknowledgements

For access to records and for photographic material our thanks to the following are expressed:

Swansea Public Library; the Gower Society; Swansea Museum; The South Wales Evening Post; The National Museum of Wales, Cardiff; The Glamorgan Records Office, Cardiff; Trinity House Depot, Swansea; Trinity House, London; Mumbles Coastguard; Bradford Barton Limited, Publishers, Cornwall, and the Royal National Lifeboat Institute.

Our thanks to Mr Graham Farr without whose kind permission and excellent volume *Wreck and Rescue in the Bristol Channel Vol II* this work would not have been as comprehensive; and to the Trustees of the estate of the late Jack Beynon whose *Eyewitness Accounts of Shipwrecks on the Gower Coast* proved extremely valuable.

Our thanks for assistance and for permissions are also due to Inspector T. E. Williams, M.B.E., H.M. Coastguard (retired), Mrs V. Fairfax, National Maritime Museum, Greenwich, Swansea Maritime Museum, Messrs Charles and Edward Harris and Mrs Rosalind Harris, Mr Gareth Mills, Mr Carl Smith, Mr Glyn Williams, R.N.L.I., and Quadrant Ltd.

Both we the publishers and the author have made every effort to trace the copyright-holders of all the photographs used in illustration. In some cases we failed to trace the original owners of such copyrights. We thank them in advance and ask that they make contact with us so that proper acknowledgement can be made in any future editions.

Contents

List of Illustrations

Frontispiece:
'Rescue at Sea' by A. Harris
Line drawings:
Alwyn Dempster-Jones

Introduction

The Industrial Revolution brought about a vast increase in the volume of shipping at the various ports around the country. The Port of Swansea was no exception, but its natural geographical barriers made the approaches dangerous to incoming and outgoing vessels. In order to make these approaches safer, a lighthouse was built on the Outer Mumbles Head in 1794. Before this date, an open wood or coal fire had probably lit the way, but this new lighthouse of proper construction and strategically positioned was a great improvement. The lighthouse still used coal as its source of power, but by 1799 an oil lantern had been introduced. In 1803 a light was placed at the end of Swansea West Pier, making the approaches to the port much more safe.

The lights made a great improvement to the situation, but the dangers along the coast remained, and vessels were regularly lost — particularly along the South Gower Coast. In 1846, on October 1st, (probably due to the loss of the steamship *City of Bristol* in Rhossili Bay six years earlier) Trinity House placed a lightship on the western end of the Helwick Sand Bank. A light was also positioned at Scarweather in 1862, Swansea tradesmen contributing towards its upkeep.

The North Coast of Gower also provided obstacles for vessels entering the Burry Estuary. Sand banks in the mouth of the estuary between Burry Holms and the Carmarthenshire Coast, combined with very fast tides, made navigation in this area dangerous at the best of times. As well as entering the larger ports of Burry Port and Llanelli, many vessels ventured further up the mud flats as far as Cheriton, Landimore, Llanrhidian and Penclawdd. Many of these vessels came to grief and almost all were put at risk on the sand banks — due to the poor navigational aids at the entrance of the estuary.

In the early Nineteenth Century, a floating hulk showing a light was positioned in Broughton Bay, and in 1854, a lighthouse was constructed on piles at Whitford Point. This lighthouse was replaced by the present familiar tower in 1866. This tower remained in service until December 21st, 1921, when, due to changes in the course of the main channel, it was superceded by a smaller lighthouse on Burry Holms. The Burry Holms light was removed from service in 1966, and all that remains of it now is its concrete base. The Whitford Tower still stands, however, and has become a popular land and sea mark, although long gone is the wrought iron, copper and lead lining which once protected it from the elements. This lighthouse was manned; the keepers there would alternate every two weeks with those stationed on the light at the Llanelli Harbour entrance.

These aids to navigation improved the situation tremendously. But the dangers still existed and vessels still floundered with severe loss of life. The Port of Swansea was growing rapidly, but at this time, no official lifeboat was stationed there. The pilot and tug boats did much to render assistance to stricken vessels, but the state of affairs was clearly unsatisfactory. In 1834, the newspaper *The Cambrian* urged the necessity for obtaining a boat, and as if to emphasise the need, two vessels floundered on Mixon Sands within the month of the article. Local opinion was strongly in favour of a boat, so a petition for a lifeboat was forwarded to John Henry Vivian, the Member of Parliament for the area. The request was granted by the National Institute For The Preservation Of Life From Shipwreck as the Royal National Lifeboat Institution was then known, and a boat arrived in 1835 which was probably housed at Swansea. Difficulty was found, however, in manning the boat. It was recorded in 1851 that the boat had not even been used. In April 1856, a more modern boat was sent to Swansea; but this also, according to records, was not used for rescue work.

The overturned lifeboat 'Edward Prince of Wales' as she was found after she had gone out to assist the 'Samtampa' wrecked at Sker Point near Porthcawl on April 23rd, 1947.

The steamship 'Christina' aground off Port Talbot. The Mumbles lifeboat 'James Stevens No. 12' was wrecked whilst going to her aid on February 1st, 1903. Six lifeboatmen were drowned.

The 'Samtampa' herself, wrecked at Sker Point, Porthcawl.

In the early 1850's, the RNLI underwent reorganisation. A committee, set up by the Harbour Trust, invited the institution to establish a station either at Swansea or the Mumbles. As a result, a boat was sent to Mumbles in 1863 and a boat house completed in 1865. The boat was named *Martha and Anne,* after the two daughters of an Oxfordshire man, Michael Steel, who contributed to the overall cost. The first vessel the boat assisted was the *Duke of Northumberland,* which found herself in difficulties on December 3rd, 1863.

Many other lifeboats have since given distinguished service from Mumbles, three of which met with disaster themselves. The first disaster involved the *Wolverhampton,* which was lost in January 1883 whilst attempting to assist the barque *Admiral Prinz Adelbert* off Mumbles Head. Four of her crew were drowned.

February 1903 saw the second disaster, when the lifeboat *James Stevens No. 12* was thrown out of control against the breakwater at Aberavon Beach. She had been helping the steamtug *Christina* at the time, and six of her crew were washed overboard and drowned.

The third and worst disaster took place at Sker Point, Porthcawl, in 1947, when the steamer *Samtampa* ran aground. The lifeboat, *Edward, Prince of Wales,* was launched, and the following morning she was found overturned on the rocks off Sker. Her crew of eight had perished along with the thirty nine men who had crewed the *Samtampa.* This lifeboat, incidentally, was the first powered boat to see service from Mumbles.

The establishment of a boat at Mumbles helped put the minds of many Gower folk at ease, but many people felt that a second boat positioned further down the South Gower Coast would offer greater improvement still. During the same storm which resulted in the loss of the *Prinz Adelbert* and the Mumbles boat in 1883, the steamer *Agnes Jack* drove ashore at Porteynon Point with serious loss of life. That

The 'Surprise', wrecked 1883 (National Maritime Museum, Greenwich).

fearful storm also wrecked the *James Grey* off Tusker Rock, Porthcawl, resulting in twenty five lives being lost. The same week also saw the vessel *Surprise* meet its end at Overton Cliff, adding seven more to the list of dead. These tragic events resulted in the much awaited second boat, which was positioned at Porteynon in May 1884. The boat was named *A Daughter's Offering* by the request of the donor, and on May 10th, she was officially launched. The boat saw regular service, but in July 1906 was replaced with a new boat of the latest design. The *Janet*, as the new boat was named, did her duty at Porteynon for nearly ten years. On Saturday, January 1st, 1916, whilst returning from assisting the *S.S. Dunvegan*, she was capsized twice by heavy seas, three of her crew members being lost. A memorial to this tragic event is to be seen at Porteynon Church.

The RNLI decided not to replace the *Janet* so that the Porteynon station was abandoned. The Institution considered that the coming improvements to the Mumbles and Tenby lifeboats, together with the advent of steam power and radio, would mean that the need for a boat at Porteynon would become greatly reduced. The boathouse, complete with slipway still remains on the beach. It has since been converted into a Youth Hostel.

Many wrecks along the South Gower Coast occurred on the razor sharp rocks at the base of the cliffs where no lifeboat could reach with safety. Considering this difficulty, the Board of Trade elected to position Life Saving Apparatus Companies at strategic points along the coast, notably at Rhossili and Oxwich. These Companies manned by villagers equipped with the latest techniques in cliff-to-vessel rescue saved the lives of many crews who would surely have otherwise drowned and perished.

One cannot treat the subject of ship wrecks around the Gower Coast without mentioning the smuggling and wrecking activities which lined the pockets of many

The crew of Porteynon lifeboat

Gower folk. Not all the wrecks were the fault of the many natural geographical obstacles, and many tales are told of how vessels were lured to their doom by false lights.

One story tells of how three Customs and Excise officers rode into the village of Middleton near Rhossili one cold winter's morning. They were invited into a farm house and were given a warming measure of rum with hot water from the kettle. The men asked for more water as they thought the rum was very strong. The farmer's wife readily supplied the water, but unkown to the three men, the water was in fact hot gin! The Customs officers soon fell into a deep sleep, and whilst in that condition, all illicit goods in the neighbourhood were hidden from view. The visitors left that evening sadder and wiser men!

Another story tells of an amusing incident which occurred on Rhossili beach one

The Rhossili Lifesaving Apparatus Company 1899. (Swansea Library)

Board of Trade 'Rocket Apparatus Company' tokens distributed by its officers among those seen to have volunteered valuable assistance in rescue operations at the scene of a wrecking. These brass tokens (about the size of a 5p coin) were then presented for claim of payment at the nearest H.M. Coastguard Headquarters. (Quadrant)

night when several bodies were being washed ashore. Searching the beach for profit that night were two men who never saw eye to eye with each other, one coming from Llangennith, and the other a native of Rhossili itself. The Rhossili man, seeing the other approaching, lay down on the sand pretending to be one of the unfortunate shipwrecked souls. The Llangennith man approached and turned the body over with the intention of rifling the pockets. As the body turned however, an arm swung up and hit the man a blow to the face. The man did not stop running until he reached Llangennith.

Many Gower folk all along the Gower Coast were involved with smuggling in one way or another, if stories are to be believed. Probably the most successful band of such smugglers had their headquarters at two farms near Pennard Church. It is recorded that these farms, Great and Little Highway, were storehouses for illicit goods, and that they were the centres for distributing such goods to all parts of the country. The goods were probably landed from vessels in the Channel at Brandy Cove (hence its name) or Pwlldu, and from these coves taken up through Bishopston Valley and deposited at the farms.

This prosperous state of affairs, however, came to an end in 1804 when the Sea Fencibles, the Home Guard of those days, accompanied by Excise men patrolling the coast, spotted a vessel anchoring in Oxwich Bay. Two men came ashore from the vessel, and enquired as to where the farms could be located. The men were informed that the farms lay around the next headland at Pennard, and they then returned to the vessel. Suspicious of a landing that night, the Sea Fencibles lay in wait, and confirming their suspicions when they observed the vessel discharging the goods, followed the smugglers to the two farms. The party of seamen and those present at the farm were arrested, and nearly three thousand gallons of spirits were recovered, much of it hidden away in cellars under the kitchen floors.

Several such well-organised gangs undoubtedly operated on Gower in these early days, and probably did very well for themselves at that; for the coast with its many coves was extremely difficult to patrol constantly. A lot of Gower folk had a hand in these clandestine activities and the only people left in the dark, so to speak, were the Excise men themselves! Those who indulged in such illicit practices did so in order to add a little excitement to their otherwise uninteresting lives, and very few made any great monetary gain.

P.H.R.

The artist, David Cobb's impression of the 'William Gammon'.

The Dollar Ship

Of all the many shipwrecks which have occurred on and around the Gower Coast, probably the most well known, and perhaps the best loved, is that known locally as the Dollar Ship, wrecked during the Seventeenth Century on Rhossili Beach. This wreck has been the source of much argument, as very little is known about it. When exactly was it lost? What was its name? What became of its crew? Where was she from? Why was she reputedly carrying so much treasure? These are all questions whose answers lie deep in the sand and mud of the bay. The fact that no official record of this wreck exists, probably points to the fact that her remains were not discovered until some time after her stranding. One theory, and one which I personally believe to be true, is that she probably floundered at night, unobserved and below the low water mark. Assuming that the seas would have broken her up, all that would remain at dawn would be pieces of wreckage strewn around the beach, thus giving no indication at all of her location. For all the curious villagers could tell from the evidence, the wreck had probably occurred far out in the bay, or even in the channel itself.

Exceptionally low tides probably exposed her shattered hull years later as was the case in 1807 and 1833, when many dollars were found in the mud. In 1807, twelve pounds in weight of dollars, half dollars, and pieces of eight were recovered, some of them dating from 1625 and 1639. Similar discoveries were made in 1833, when a cannon and part of an Astrolabe, an instrument formerly used for taking altitudes, were found.

Many stories of the Dollar Ship evolved, and one tells of the late Mrs Janet Ace who lived in Overton where she died in 1888. Born in Llangennith in 1810, and known as Jennie Grove, she worked on the farm of Mr Bevan in that same parish.

It is recorded that she often told of the great gale and low ebb of 1883 when the ship became exposed. She described in her stories how Mr Bevan once returned from the beach carrying a bag of dollars — 'As large as he could carry' — which he tipped out on the floor of the farm kitchen.

A house called Dollar Cot in Llangennith is believed to be another link with the wreck, as it is thought that the house was built from the proceeds of dollar finds.

The many unanswered questions surrounding the Dollar Ship are made more complicated by the fact that gold doubloons and moidores were discovered in Blue Pool Bay in 1770 and more again in 1840. Local fishermen have found the gold amongst rocks and pools, and these discoveries point to the loss of a vessel near the bay, probably a vessel of Portuguese origin. The fact that the discoveries were made near the high water mark, suggests that she grounded near the shore, giving her crew a good chance of survival.

Stories also tell of how a convoy of three ships ran into a storm. Two of the vessels reputedly were driven ashore, one grounding near Spanish Rocks, whilst the other was driven before the wind as far as Llanrhidian marsh. This vessel, of which there is little evidence, was supposedly carrying gold bullion which was recovered intact. The convoy was said to have comprised a Spanish galleon escorted by two other ships, whose mission was to carry the dowry of a Spanish Princess who was to marry an English Nobleman. This story, however, probably grew from the fact that at about the same time, Catherine Braganza was betrothed to Charles II, and in 1662 married him. Her dowry was most probably brought by way of the English Channel, and it is popularly believed that the orangery at Margam owes its origin to Catherine's dowry, washed ashore after a shipwreck.

Records show that a Portuguese vessel was wrecked on a sand bank ten miles from

Swansea in 1666, and although this wreck probably accounts for the gold doubloons, it is doubtfully the Dollar Ship or the Portuguese dowry, as all treasure recovered was of Spanish origin.

The confusion over these two ships is the result of their loss having occurred in the same year: 1666. A letter, however, dated March 21st, 1697 from an Alexander Trotter to Sir Edward Mansel concerning iron scrap from the vessel, gives rise to further doubt: that the Dollar Ship was wrecked some thirty years later — in 1696.

Several dollars from Rhossili beach are still in existence bearing the insignia of King Phillip, but more exciting is the fact that many more still lie buried waiting to be found. It is nearly 150 years since the last reported discovery during which time the vessel has probably settled further into the mud.

Caesar 1760

During the middle of the Eighteenth Century, it was reported that a war vessel had been wrecked near Pwlldu. Reports of the incident conflicted greatly as to the number of dead, but all told of many bodies strewn along the shore. The vessel broke up quickly, and the death toll must have been high — as the bodies were buried in a common grave on the Eastern slopes of the headland. This locality is still known to this day as Gravesend. The ship was carrying a large number of pressed men battened down below decks. These men probably made up the majority of dead, and it is said that only one of the pressed men actually survived. Stories abound of how he was hidden and looked after by a local man, Dick Meyrick, until he could safely return to his native Devon. Sometime later Meyrick was conscripted for the Militia, but lacking the statutory fifty pounds necessary to buy himself out, he was obliged to serve.

Meyrick was posted to Plymouth where, by a remarkable chance, he met up with the man to whom he had given shelter. His old friend put up the money for Meyrick's release, and consequently Meyrick made an early return to his Gower home.

Records do not indicate the exact location of the wreck, nor indeed the vessel's name. It is unlikely, however, that a wreck of such magnitude could pass unrecorded. The loss of one military vessel is recorded in the Customs Papers for December 1760. It possibly refers to the same incident. In the report the vessel's name is given as *Caesar,* an Admiralty tender. The Captain and his Lieutenant survived, and the Captain was ordered to pay the local folk for disposing of the many bodies. The number of bodies recovered was given as sixty eight.

Among the weapons recorded were:

44 muskets
31 damaged musket barrels
10 stock pieces
27 pistols
50 swords
23 scabbards
7 pole axes

There is evidence that recoveries of munitions were being made as late as September 1761, when a Mr George Knight of Swansea sought authority to forward eight guns salvaged from the wreck to Bristol.

La Concorde 1815

The French vessel *La Concorde,* on route from Montpelier for Antwerp ran aground in the Burry Estuary on December 1st, 1815. Westerly gales had blown her severely from her intended course, and when the tide eventually ebbed leaving the hulk stranded, local villagers waded out into the mud and stole most of her cargo of spirits. Before leaving, the mob set fire to the remains of the vessel completely destroying it. Customs and Excise officials tried to intervene, but the villagers outnumbered them greatly. Troops were called in in an effort to recover the cargo, but to no avail.

Bounty Hall 1819

The *Bounty Hall,* a seven hundred ton vessel owned by the East India Company, grounded on Llanmadoc sands on December 19th, 1819. Where exactly she came ashore is not recorded, but she suffered little, if any, damage. Villagers soon arrived at the scene, and all gave a hand in discharging the cargo of rice, spirits and sugar. The vessel was later refloated. It was reported at the time that five days after her unfortunate arrival, the Swansea Cavalry were detailed to the scene to safeguard the cargo from the looters. They found the cargo neatly stacked on the burrows. The villagers were congratulated on the considerable restraint they had shown in not stealing any of the foodstuffs!

Amethyst 1833

During the later months of 1833, severe weather decided the Master of the brigantine *Amethyst* to seek shelter in the Bristol Channel. At the time, she had been sailing for Quebec, having left Liverpool several days earlier. Bad luck prevailed, however, and the vessel floundered just outside Swansea, probably on the Mixon Sands. At this time no lifeboat existed either at Swansea or Mumbles, but a Swansea Pilot, John Mitchell, and his crew managed to save the crew of the *Amethyst* after performing a difficult and dangerous rescue.

Margaret 1834

On November 1st, 1834, the Maltese barque *Margaret* sailed from Swansea with a cargo of coal for Alexandria. The wind filled her sails for five days and she made good progress reaching a position approximately 120 miles South West from the channel. On the sixth day, however, her luck changed and she ran into a severe gale — suffering heavy damage. The winds tore away the main top sail, and the fore and main yards were lost overboard. The severe buffeting opened up leaks in her hull, and she quickly began to fill with water. The crew manned the pumps continuously, and with great difficulty managed to stem the rise in the water level. The *Margaret*'s Master tried to make for Milford Haven, but on arrival at a point six miles off shore, the land became obscured by a haze, and so a course was set to return to Swansea.

On the night of November 8th, the crew observed a light which they correctly took to be Mumbles lighthouse. The anchor was dropped and it was decided to wait until

The 'Amethyst' (National Maritime Museum, Greenwich).

daylight before an attempt be made to reach the shore. Sometime later the tide ebbed, and the *Margaret* found herself on the Mixon Sands. More anchor cable was given out and the vessel managed to get herself refloated in deep water. The Captain and four of his crew took the vessel's boat and managed to reach the shore safely in the early hours of the morning.

Two steam tugs were sent out to the *Margaret* with a relief crew of twenty men, and her original crew taken off. The relief crew took over the pumps and managed to beach the vessel at Mumbles where her badly damaged hull was temporarily repaired.

Mary Ann 1834

Nine days after the beaching of the *Margaret,* the schooner *Mary Ann* from Wexford ran into a gale. She had been on her way home from Cardiff with a cargo of coal, but was soon driven back before the wind on to the Mixon. Her crew and several passengers were saved by Coastguards, but the vessel was lost.

The loss of these last three vessels, the *Amethyst,* the *Margaret* and the *Mary Anne,* led to the decision to establish a lifeboat at Swansea.

City of Bristol 1840

During the night of the 17th, 18th, November 1840, the paddle steamer *City of Bristol* grounded on Rhossili sands several hundred yards North West of Diles Lake. The steam packet had set out from Waterford the previous day in stormy weather,

City of Bristol. (Gower Society)

and her Mastern Captain Stacey, set a course across Carmarthen Bay. The wind later subsided a little, but the seas were still running high and Captain Stacey decided to seek shelter in Rhossili Bay until the weather became more favourable.

Steaming through the darkness, white water was suddenly observed on her larboard side, and with a sickening thud she grounded on the beach. Engines were reversed, but the powerful steam paddles failed to refloat her and she turned broadside on to the pounding seas. It would have been suicide to have tried to launch a lifeboat, and the crew were forced to remain aboard hoping that the steamer would refloat itself on the flood tide. Records differ as to the exact number of crew aboard, but they agree that the number was between twenty five and thirty four men — two women and a child being passengers.

The end of the *City of Bristol* came at about midnight, when the heavy seas broke her hull into three, spilling man and beast into the water. No moon shone that night, which made rescue operations difficult. Villagers, attracted by cries of help, crowded the beach, but were unable to do anything until the unfortunate men and beasts materialised from the darkness. The terrible reality of that night only became apparent the following morning when the bodies washed ashore. After the terrible ordeal, it was realised that only two persons had managed to reach the shore alive: one a carpenter, Thomas Hamlier, and the other a cattleman taking passage with his livestock, a common enough practice on the Irish packets. The two survivors were taken care of by William Tucker at the Kings Head in Llangennith, where later the inquest on the tragedy was held. The vessel's cargo had consisted of 280 pigs, 15 head of cattle and 370 barrels of oats. The animals fared better than the crew and passengers, with 72 pigs and four head of cattle surviving. The animals were cared for at Cwm Ivy by Mr George Holland, a Lloyds agent.

Such livestock, it should be noted, often contributed to such disasters at sea. With open and exposed pens located on deck, heavy seas often drove the beasts wild with panic, thus affecting the vessel's stability. This state of affairs was corrected years later, however, when larger vessels enabled the pens to be positioned below deck. The verdict of the inquest on the death of Captain Stacey was recorded as follows:—

That the said John Stacey on the night of November 18th, 1840, being in a certain vessel called the *City of Bristol,* and the said vessel by the violence of the winds and waves, became stranded and wrecked on Llangennith sands in the parish of Llangennith in the County of Glamorgan, by means whereof the said John Stacey was then and there accidentally, casually, and by misfortune thrown into the sea, and in the waters thereof, was then and there suffocated and drowned.

Knowing exactly where the beach was positioned was made very difficult, as at that time no light was placed on the treacherous Helwick Sand Bank, nor was there a light on Burry Holms. In 1846 however, six years later, a light vessel was positioned at Helwick, possibly as a result of the loss of the *City of Bristol.* At the subsequent inquest, a representative of the Bristol General Steam Navigation Company, who were the owners, paid tribute to the villagers for their assistance given on that terrible night.

Rothery Castle 1847

The new light positioned at the Helwick sand bank several years after the loss of the *City of Bristol,* did however cause a tragic incident itself, probably in the year 1847. It is thought that by some mischance, the Master of the vessel *Rothery Castle* mistook the light for that of Mumbles. Homeward bound with a cargo from the Orient, he turned the vessel, as he thought, into Mumbles Bay. The vessel struck the sandbank and was smashed to pieces — the entire crew being lost.

Arietta 1848

Although a lifeboat was established in the Port of Swansea in 1835, difficulty was found in manning her. The pilot and tug boats continued to do much of the rescue work. On November 27th, 1848 the barque *Arietta* of Sunderland, returning from Cuba was driven by rough weather onto the Mixon Sands. She began to break up. Heavy seas washed the Second Mate overboard, but the remaining crew, fourteen in all, boarded the vessel's boat and were very fortunate in being picked up by the *Dragon Fly,* a paddle tug. It was doubtful if the small boat could have survived much longer in those heavy seas, and even if it had, there were few places along the coast where it could have made a successful landing in the pounding surf.

Margaret 1850

Many storms have unleashed themselves at the Gower, but one of the worst occurred in August 1850. The day the storm broke, the schooner *Margaret,* owned and commanded by Captain Thomas of Rhossili, lay at anchor in Rhossili Bay. Captain Thomas was betrothed to a Miss Beynon of Pitton, and several of the Beynon family were invited aboard the vessel. Soon after boarding, the wind rose and the vessel's small boat could not be launched to land the party ashore. The wind was South West, and Captain Thomas in fear of being blown towards the shore, decided to put to sea. He sent his guests below deck and sailed out into Carmarthen Bay in an attempt to reach Tenby. A full gale developed, and several of the villagers fearing the safety of the vessel went to the cliff top, but by now could see nothing of the vessel. The wind proved to be of such strength, that the villagers had to get down on their knees and crawl for fear of being blown over the cliff.

The *Margaret* did not manage to reach Tenby as the wind had now turned West. Instead, the vessel was driven onto the sands at Burry Holmes, and at high tide found herself on the beach at Broughton Bay. She had lost both masts, and had suffered other serious damage. She was eventually refloated and lashed to two empty barges and later repaired, but she was never seen at Rhossili again.

The Beynon family all landed ashore safely, but all were very frightened and very thankful to be alive. The storm, incidentally, wrought havoc on the Gower farmsteads, and brought near starvation to many people in the area.

Catherine Jenkins 1856

The various smelting works for Copper in Swansea during the early Eighteenth Century, obtained much of their crude ore from mines throughout Britain and Ireland. The copper produced was of a low quality, and the Swansea smelters began drawing up contracts with local ship owners, willing to venture as far as Cuba and Peru where rich ore lay in abundance. As a result, Swansea vessels began to sail the 'Cuba Run.'

The *Catherine Jenkins*, an ore trader of 350 tons, was a regular visitor to these foreign shores. She was built in 1835 for William Jenkins, a well-known local businessman and ship owner. Soon after his death, however, the vessel was sold by his widow to Messrs Ord of Sunderland who operated vessels from Swansea. The vessel had been custom built for the 'Cuba Run', and for several years had made many successful crossings without serious incident. Her last voyage to Cuba commenced in the Autumn of 1855, the voyage being planned so as to avoid the Summer hurricane season. Mathew Hodge was in command, the total crew consisting of sixteen men.

The vessel left Swansea, sailed down channel, cleared the Scilly Isles, and crossed the Bay of Biscay without harm. A good passage was made to Madeira, and when she reached the Canaries the North East trade winds caught her sails and sped her across the Atlantic to Barbados. Her first landfall was at an island just off Guadeloupe, named Desalda. From this point she sailed through the Antigua Passage along to the Jamaica-Hispaniola Channel, and then on to Santiago.

Whilst at anchor in Santiago Bay the troubles which were to plague the *Catherine Jenkins* took over events. The crew were taken ill with Yellow Fever, five of them dying from the disease. The vessel's schedule was badly interrupted, and to make matters worse, difficulty was found in bringing the vessel's complement to full strength again. Eventually her cargo was loaded and secured, and reluctantly Captain Hodge sailed for the return trip with a crew of only eleven men.

Already severely delayed, Hodge decided not to go with the wind through the channel between Cuba and Hispaniola, as this would have meant that the vessel would have had to combat the strong trade winds. To do so would have meant tacking back and forth for weeks before making a decent passage. The vessel sailed from Santiago Bay on Christmas Eve and headed for Cape San Antonio and the Florida Strait. Whilst in the Strait, heavy currents almost drove her against the many reefs there, but she managed to escape unscathed. Clearing the Florida Strait, she sailed along the American coast as far as Newfoundland where she caught the Westerly winds.

The *Catherine Jenkins* reached Lundy on the night of Thursday, February 7th. The darkness of night was made worse by a thick fog, and at about 3 a.m. the Second Mate informed the Captain that breakers could be heard ahead. Before corrective manoeuvers could be made, the vessel struck just off Lucas Bay and began to settle.

The crew launched the small boat. They all clambered aboard. A heavy swell was running, and this, coupled with the fact that the boat had only two oars, caused the boat to capsize. Thompson and Hughes, the two mates, Thomas Harris, an ordinary seaman, and the Portuguese cook, were the only crew members to survive. The unfortunate men who lost their lives included Captain Hodge and four Swansea men.

At 9 a.m. the next day, the *Catherine Jenkins* lost her battle with the heavy breakers and broke up. Her cargo of ore was later manhandled to the grass slopes on the shore, and eventually taken to the smelting works. For many years after this incident, grass and other vegetation was loath to grow at the spot where the cargo was salvaged, as so much corrosive deposit had drained into the soil from the ore.

It is interesting to note that soon after the 'Cuba Run' had become established in Swansea, Santiago became known as the 'Swansea Cemetry'. Few vessels entering her bay escaped 'Yellow Jack' (Yellow Fever), and it was reported that in January of 1845, twelve vessels arriving from Cuba had all suffered losses. In 1866, Swansea found itself at the mercy of this disease.

Villiers 1861

The 142 ton *Villiers* of London left Cardiff on September 1st, 1861 to commence her voyage to Alicante with a cargo of coal. Approaching Gower the following night, the weather turned bad and her Master, James Pill, decided to shelter in the Mumbles Roads. Soon after eleven o'clock, the vessel struck the Mixon Sands and quickly began to settle. Four members of the eight-man crew took to the boats. At the subsequent enquiry four days later, Captain Pill maintained that he had not authorised the launching of this boat. The boat with its four occupants had capsized near Mumbles Head, two of the men being drowned; the other two clinging to the upturned boat until saved. The remaining crew members aboard the *Villiers* took shelter in the topmost rigging, and nearly eight hours later were rescued by the steam tug *Beaufort*. The loss of this vessel, however, did have its usefulness. At the enquiry it was agreed that a lightship be placed upon the Scarweather sands. The Admirality Board agreed to position such a vessel, providing the Swansea traders would contribute towards its upkeep.

As one sixth of all United Kingdom vessels navigated the Bristol Channel at that time, this was agreed upon by the businessmen of Swansea. The light was positioned where it now lies.

A young lad by the name of Peachy, one of the survivors of the *Villiers*, made the local headlines by surviving three shipwrecks in the space of six months. In the early months of 1861 he was aboard the barque *Orissa* when it sank off Cape St Verde on March 20th. With other survivors from the vessel he was landed at Liverpool where he joined the *Villiers*. Landed at Swansea after the loss of the *Villiers*, he signed aboard the barque *Fanny*. This vessel had just completed an expensive overhaul, but on October 22nd she was completely destroyed by fire at sea.

Even this third disaster did not deter young Peachy from venturing to sea yet again.

Duke of Northumberland 1863

Several vessels were approaching the Port of Swansea on the evening of December 3rd, 1863 when a North Westerly gale sprang up. Arriving from Cuba with a cargo of copper ore was the barque *Duke of Northumberland*. She lowered her anchor to avoid drifting, but the anchor cable parted and her mainsails were lost. The vessel drifted out of control and eventually ran aground upon a sand bank in the bay. The Mumbles lifeboat *Martha and Anne* was launched and stood by the stricken vessel through most of the night. The lifeboat eventually took off the vessel's seventeen crew members and one passenger.

Francis and Ann 1865

Overton cliffs, the graveyard of many unfortunate vessels, claimed yet another victim on January 26th, 1865. Heavy seas forced the vessel *Francis and Ann* into Overton Mere where she quickly broke up against the razor sharp rocks. Her hull smashed open, and her cargo of oranges spilled into the surging seas where they were scattered far afield, giving the coast an unusual splash of colour. This vessel became locally known as the 'Orange Vessel'.

Rene 1866

The arrival one night in January 1866 of a wet, sorry-looking black retriever in the village of Overton, caused villagers to hurry to the cliff top. Peering over the edge they saw the remains of the French barque *Rene* being methodically smashed to pieces by the heavy seas. The vessel totally disintegrated on the rocks, and five of her crew lost their lives. In a pool near Kilboidy a heavy iron stancheon remains as the only relic of this vessel.

The Burry Estuary Wrecks 1868

One of the worst incidents of multiple shipwreck on the coast of Great Britain, excluding of course military engagements, took place on the North coast of the Gower Peninsula at the mouth of the Burry Estuary on the night of January 22nd, 1868. Several days prior to this date, the Gower had been ravaged by Westerly gales, but on the 22nd the winds had blown themselves out and the sea became calm. The disaster which was about to occur involved vessels setting out from the Port of Llanelli, their Masters and crews happy in the knowledge that the fierce Westerly gales had at last abated.

Llanelli in those days was a busy little port, even though the sand bar at its approaches proved a somewhat dangerous obstacle. It was indeed this sand bar, on that calm, practically windless evening, which was to bring doom to many of the vessels as they set out on the ebb tide. Although the wind had abated almost to nothing, unknown to the Masters of the vessels the bar was still in tremendous swell. The vessels, nineteen in all, proceeded down the Burry Estuary in convoys of four bow to stern, and towed by tugs. The vessels were the *Eliza* of Jersey, the *Mary Anne* of Amlwch, the *St Catherine* of Fay, the *Amethyst* of Dublin, the *Huntress* of Workington, the *Jeune Celine* of Jersey, the *Ann* of Barnstaple, the *Sophie* of Regneville, the Pilot cutter *Ceres,* and several other small ships. The whole convoy ranged from 20 tons upwards to 400 tons.

Things began to go wrong soon after the tugboats cast off their towlines. The sea was running a heavy swell, and there being hardly any wind to catch the sails, the vessels all began to drift. Some drifted on to the bar and were severely buffeted by the sea against the sand. Those which managed to be swept off the bar found that the inrush of water through their stoved-in hulls was far too much for the pumps to handle and they soon began to sink. The vessels which missed the bar completely, found themselves driven onto the beaches where the heavy seas soon began to break them up. In a very short time, four ships were on the beach at Llanmadoc only yards from each other, and five or six lay wrecked in Broughton bay.

Control of the vessels was such an impossible task, that several of them collided. Captain Thomas Roberts, Master and owner of the Llanelli brigantine *The Brothers,* found his vessel with several others of the same tow, in a position which he himself thought was clear of the bar. His towline was cast off, and soon afterwards, to his horror, he realised that he was drifting towards the shore. At eleven o'clock at night, *The Brothers* struck the bar. Shortly afterwards the crew observed another vessel, which they recognised as the *Roscius* of Llanelli, approaching them completely out of control. The vessels collided, the *Roscius* being badly holed. Her crew together with the pilot, eight men in all, jumped safely to the deck of *The Brothers* whilst the two vessels were interlocked. Another vessel, the brigantine *Jeune Celine* was soon observed, her Master desperately calling for help.

The 'Roscius', wrecked 1868 (National Maritime Meusum, Greenwich).

The 'Eliza', 1868 (National Maritime Museum, Greenwich).

The 'Ann', 1868 (National Maritime Museum, Greenwich).

The 'Mary Fanny', 1868 (National Maritime Museum, Greenwich).

The Brothers at last cleared the bank, left the *Roscius* to the mercy of the seas and managed to get afloat again in deep water. Captain Roberts decided to drop anchor, but all too soon realised that too much water was seeping through his vessel's battered hull. The anchor cable was cut, and the vessel allowed to beach herself. Her crew, along with the men from the *Roscius* decided to seek refuge on the hulk lightship in Broughton Bay, where they found the crews of several other vessels clinging on for dear life. In the darkness the men could hear cries of help coming from vessels out on the bar, vessels which were slowly breaking apart, spilling their crews into the dark seas.

A survivor from the *Ann* of Barnstaple related how the heavy seas had knocked the vessel's mainmast out when she was at the Burry Estuary approaches. The vessel drifted into Broughton Bay along with several others. 'When we left Llanelli, we thought it was all smooth, as it had been calm all day.'

When daylight finally appeared, it disclosed the gruesome fate of the convoy. Llanmadoc and Broughton sands were strewn with wreckage and cargo, and even worse, many bodies lay in stark evidence upon the yellow sand. Several of the vessels were salvaged and one, the *Elizabeth* of Barnstaple, put in to Tenby severely battered after her ordeal.

Eighteen lives were lost that night, and of vessels lost with all hands were the *Waterfly,* the *Jeune Celine,* the *Huntress,* the *Amethyst* and the *Mary Fanny*. The *Mary Fanny* was later salvaged from where she ran aground in Rhossili and was rebuilt. She sailed for many years afterwards until she was sunk by a German U-boat in 1918.

Triton 1873

On August 29th, 1873, the Prussian barque *Triton* left Swansea bound for Eckerneforde in Germany loaded with salt. The vessel reached Lundy where heavy seas and strong winds made the captain decide to turn back to Mumbles for shelter. The gale became worse, and the vessel drove against the Mixon Sands at 4 a.m. and began to break up. The *Triton* had a crew of nine, two of whom launched the vessel's boat against the captain's orders. The boat, however, capsized soon after leaving the ship and the two crew members drowned. The *Digby Grand,* a Swansea paddle tug, managed to take five crew members off the stricken vessel, but only the lifeboat *Wolverhampton* was able to get in close enough in order to pick up the last survivors. For this difficult rescue, the Emperor of Germany gave the Coxswain of the *Wolverhampton* a pair of binoculars, and to the remaining lifeboat crew he gave sums of money.

Sarah Ann 1879

On January 8th, 1879, the barque *Sarah Ann* sailed into Swansea Bay, outward bound for Montevideo with a cargo of coal. She was caught by an East-South-Easterly gale, which soon caused the seas to crash over her decks. Unfortunately, there was not sufficient time to batten down the hatches properly, and water soon began to fill the inside of the hull. The ten crew members were picked up by the lifeboat *Wolverhampton,* and soon afterwards the *Sarah Ann* floundered and sank.

Mary Stenhouse 1879

In 1879, on a dark and stormy night, the *Mary Stenhouse* ran aground on Rhossili beach at a point near the old rectory. She was being towed at the time from Liverpool to Swansea, and whether the vessel lost or cut her cable when she found herself in difficulties was never known. The coastguard at Rhossili at the time was Mr W. H. Betts, and with himself in charge, the Rhossili Life Saving Apparatus Company quickly set up their equipment. The first rocket they fired missed the vessel, and when the smoke and heat had subsided, the rescuers found to their dismay that the rocket tube had dislodged itself and had fallen over the cliff top. Precious time was spent searching for the tube, and eventually it was located rolling about in the surf. The second shot was more successful and landed aboard the vessel. A line was run out, and soon afterwards a man was brought ashore by Breeches Buoy. He asked his rescuers if a boat had been found, and it was later learnt that when the vessel had grounded upon the beach, several members of the crew had launched a boat. Ten men and the Captain's wife had boarded, but the heavy seas broke the boat to pieces, with all occupants drowning. The ten remaining crew members, together with the carpenter's wife, had remained aboard and were subsequently rescued using the Breeches Buoy.

The following morning, a Mr G. Gibbs of Overton rode by horse to Llanelli. He managed to get a tug out to the vessel, and manoeuvering alongside, the tug managed to put one of its crew aboard with a line. A tow line was run out, and eventually the vessel was towed out into the bay.

Her crew watched her being towed away from the shore and around Worms Head. Standing in the bay was the tug which had towed her from Liverpool, her crew also watching as the Llanelli tug made the *Mary Stenhouse* her prize. The vessel was towed to Swansea without further mishap, and all that remained to remind her crew and the villagers of the incident was the scattered remains of the lifeboat and several bodies. It was later learnt that the Llanelli tug crew obtained a handsome sum for the salvage.

It is interesting to note that the *Mary Stenhouse* was the first vessel the Rhossili Life Saving Apparatus Company had ever attended at Rhossili Sands. The Company at that time had only had one practice drill before the incident occurred.

Corea 1880

A strong South Westerly gale blew hard against the barque *Corea* of Boston U.S.A. on February 10th, 1880. In heavy seas she ran aground on the Green Grounds. She struck the Grounds with such force that she lost her false keel, so the Master of the vessel decided to abandon ship. The boats were lowered, but as soon as they hit the water they were smashed to pieces by the force of the waves. The Mumbles lifeboat managed to get in close enough to remove the crew. Several lifeboatmen boarded the vessel when she was later towed by tug into Swansea.

Cresswell 1881

In 1881 the Coastguard at Rhossili was informed that a vessel had run ashore at the foot of the cliffs at Paviland. The information given to him, led him to believe that the crew had managed to reach the shore in the vessel's own boat. The Coastguard, acting upon this information, went alone to the scene of the wreck.

Upon arrival, he found that some of the crew had indeed managed to reach the shore, but there were others still aboard the vessel which by now was beginning to break up.

He returned to Rhossili and called out the Rescue Company, and upon reaching the wreck found that it had only one mast remaining. The Coastguard and his men quickly set up their equipment and successfully fired a rocket aboard the vessel. A Breeches Buoy was run out, and the remaining crew brought safely ashore. As the rescue was being performed, one of the crew members from the vessel was seen to be lashing a large chest to the rails of the ship. It was later learnt that the man concerned was the vessel's carpenter. He had been trying to save his precious tools. The last man to leave the vessel had great difficulty in entering the Buoy, and upon arrival ashore, had equal difficulty in getting out again. He cursed and swore at the coastguard and his crew for the uncomfortable journey, and upon undressing, revealed for all to see, three suits which he had worn in order to save them, thus restricting his own movements.

Soon after the crew had been brought safely ashore, the vessel finally gave up its battle with the sea and fell apart. In less than an hour from the time of rescue, all that could be seen of her were pieces of driftwood and other items of wreckage bobbing about on the water's surface.

Agnes Jack 1883

At five hours after midnight on January 27th, 1883 there started to blow one of the most fearsome South-Westerly gales ever to be experienced on Gower. The gale claimed a total of forty eight lives, including four of the crew of the

Wolverhampton, the Mumbles lifeboat. This lifeboat, it should be noted, was lost whilst assisting the barque *Admiral Prinz Adelbert* off Mumbles Head, and was the first of three lifeboats from Mumbles to be lost whilst at duty.

Within thirty minutes of the storm breaking, lights could be seen and cries of for help heard at Porteynon Point. Villagers hurried to the water's edge, but in the pitch blackness, they could see nothing except the occasional light. It was obvious that some vessel was in distress, and word was speedily sent to the Oxwich rescue crews, but it was some time later that they arrived. As daylight started to break across the morning sky, the outline of a ship could be seen. By this time the tide was at its highest and the gale-force winds sent breakers crashing over her decks. As the light steadily improved, those who were watching noticed that some of the crew had reached the relative safety of the yard arms and rigging, and were grimly holding on to them to save their lives. The villagers could do nothing to help. When the Oxwich Rocket Company arrived, their attempts to fire a line aboard the vessel were thwarted by the heavy winds. It was decided to wait until the tide had ebbed somewhat before another attempt was made, and soon after ten o'clock the Rhossili crew arrived. The two rescue crews edged their way out along the rocks. A single rocket was fired, but like the others, fell short because of the strength of the wind. Another attempt was prepared, but with a crack, the vessel's foremast collapsed, spilling its human leeches into the pounding seas. None of the crew reached the shore alive. It was later discovered that the vessel was the *Agnes Jack* which had left Sardinia bound for Llanelli carrying six hundred tons of silver-bearing copper ore. It is recorded that the vessel had arrived in the Burry Estuary the previous day but was late to catch the tide into Llanelli. Her Master decided to shelter in the Mumbles Roads, and on the evening of the 26th, with a pilot aboard, sailed down the South coast of the Gower in order to catch the flood tide into Llanelli. Records show that on that particular night, the tide turned at 2.45 a.m., so the vessel could not have been wrecked later than 3 a.m. which fact caused some uncertainty at the subsequent board of enquiry. The *Agnes Jack,* it was maintained, struck the rocks at Porteynon at low ebb tide before the storm had started to blow. There were indications, albeit disputed, that she had turned back up channel, which added to the mystery. It was discovered later that in all, eighteen men had perished, five of whom had tried to reach the shore in the vessel's small boat. The vessel's boiler can sometimes still be seen at low water.

Admiral Prinz Adelbert 1883

Only a few hours earlier from the time the drama of the *Agnes Jack* was being acted out at Porteynon, similar scenes were taking place at Mumbles. The barque *Admiral Prinz Adelbert,* with a complement of sixteen, was bound for Swansea from Rochefort carrying nearly a thousand tons of pitwood. The vessel was in difficulties due to the loss of her spars and sails as a result of a rough passage. The vessel passed the light at Lundy, and on approaching Swansea hoisted signals requesting a pilot. Her signals were not answered, but the Swansea paddle tug *Flying Scud,* seeing her obvious distress, offered to take her in tow for a fee of five hundred pounds. Captain Ludwig Leibaner, the Master of the *Prinz Adelbert,* thought this sum to be scandalous, but as it was obvious that he could not manage to reach port without assistance, finally agreed to the sum. A nine inch hawser was attached, and the barque was taken in tow, but after only fifty minutes this hawser parted. A second hawser snapped almost immediately, and the vessel drifted towards the shore. Both anchors were dropped, but heavy seas caused the vessel to pitch and roll

The Mumbles lifeboat 'Wolverhampton' shown damaged after being capsized and thrown amongst rocks whilst attempting to assist the barque 'Admiral Prinz Adelbert' in January 1883

heavily, and forty five minutes later one anchor chain parted and the other began to drag. The vessel was pushed towards the shore, and finally against the rocks West of the light house at approximately 9 a.m. on the 26th. The foremast collapsed, and in doing so dragged down both the Main and Mizzen. Rocket apparatus had been erected as a precaution, but the vessel was well out of range at the point where she had struck.

The Mumbles lifeboat *Wolverhampton* was summoned, and whilst its crew, assisted by many of the villagers, struggled to launch the boat, the chief Coastguard tried to dissuade the Coxswain from taking the boat to sea in such conditions. He told the Coxswain, 'It's hell I tell you,' only to be answered by 'Well, hell it shall be.' Three attempts were made to launch the lifeboat, but eventually she managed to get under way. It was said by one old time-beaten witness that the Coxswain should never have taken so many married men with him, when there were plenty of single men eager to help. In all fairness to the Coxswain though, he took with him in his crew four of his sons and one son-in-law. The lifeboat battled every inch of its way to the barque, and to the spectators ashore it seemed to be swallowed up by the sea on several occasions as it entered deep troughs in the mountainous seas.

The boat passed through the Inner Sound between the lighthouse and the mainland, through which the sea was running fast due to the ebb, and eventually reached the wreck at approximately 10 a.m. She was unable to approach the vessel from her lee-side due to the rocks and had to swing outside, anchor, and approach on her cable. The treacherous conditions made it impossible for the lifeboat to approach close enough to be of any use, but a crew member on the ship then had the idea of throwing a lifebelt overboard with a line attached. The bow man on the *Wolverhampton* hooked the belt, and soon, by means of the line, the lifeboat was alongside.

Two crew members from the barque had been successfully transferred when the lifeboat's cable parted. Immediately the pounding seas hurled her against the wreck, and the force of the impact was such that one of the lifeboatmen was hurled onto the deck of the barque. Huge waves smashed over the lifeboat overturning her twice. She was driven over the rocks, and soon became a wreck herself on the side of the island on which the lighthouse stood. Of the thirteen lifeboatmen, four were drowned along with the carpenter from the barque. The remaining crew from the *Wolverhampton* and two seamen from the barque were badly hurt as they were washed over the razor sharp rocks. Two of the men were saved by the memorable courage of the two daughters of the lighthouse keeper, Abraham Ace. Miss Jessie Ace waded out into the deep water over the slippery weed covered rocks, and close behind her was her sister, a Mrs Wright. Together they flung their shawls to the seamen, and managed to drag them to safety. Their brave actions are commemorated in the poem 'The Women of Mumbles Head', by Clement Scott:-

The Women of Mumbles Head

Bring, novelists, your note-book! bring dramatists, your pen!
And I'll tell you a simple story of what women do for men.
It's only the tale of a lifeboat, of the dying and the dead,
Of a terrible storm and shipwreck that happened off Mumbles Head!
Maybe you have travelled in Wales, sir, and know it North and South;
Maybe you are friends with the 'natives' that dwell at Oystermouth;
It happened, no doubt, that from Bristol you've crossed in a casual way,
And have sailed your yacht in the Summer in the blue of Swansea Bay.

Well! it isn't like that in the Winter, when the lighthouse stands alone,
In the teeth of Atlantic breakers that foam on its face of stone;
It wasn't like that when the hurricane blew, and the storm-bell tolled, or when
There was news of a wreck, and the lifeboat launched, and a desperate cry for men.
When in the world did the Coxswain shirk? a brave old salt was he!
Proud to the bone of four strong lads as ever tasted the sea.
Welshmen all to the lungs and loins, who, about that coast, 'twas said,
Have saved some hundred lives a piece — at a shilling or so a head.

So the father launched the lifeboat, in the teeth of the tempest's roar,
And he stood like a man at the rudder, with an eye on his boys at the oar.
Out to the wreck went the father! out to the wreck went the sons!
Leaving the weeping of women, and booming of signal guns,
Leaving the mother who loved them, and the girls that the sailors love,
Going to death for duty, and trusting to God above!
Do you murmur a prayer, my brothers, when cosy and safe in bed,
For men like these, who are ready to die for a wreck off Mumbles Head?

It didn't go well with the lifeboat! 'twas a terrible storm that blew!
And it snapped the rope in a second that was flung to the drowning crew;
And then the anchor parted — 'twas a tussle to keep afloat!
But the father stuck to the rudder, and the boys to the brave old boat.
Then at last on the poor doom'd lifeboat, a wave broke mountains high!
'God help us now,' said the father. 'It's over, my lads! Goodbye.'
Half of the crew swam shoreward, half to the sheltered caves,
But father and sons were fighting death in the foam of the angry waves.

Up at a lighthouse window two women beheld the storm,
And saw in the boiling breakers a figure — a fighting form,
It might be a grey-haired father, then the women held their breath,
It might be a fair-haired brother, who was having a round with death;
It might be a lover, a husband, whose kisses were on the lips
Of the women whose love is the life of men going down to the sea in ships.
They had seen the launch of the lifeboat, they had seen the worst, and more,
Then, kissing each other, these women went down from the lighthouse, straight to shore.

There by the rocks on the breakers these sisters, hand in hand,
Beheld once more that desperate man who struggled to reach the land.
'Twas only aid he wanted to help him across the wave,
But what are a couple of women with only a man to save?
What are a couple of women? well more than three craven men,
Who stood by the shore with chattering teeth, refusing to stir — and then
Off went the women's shawls, sir; in a second they're torn and rent,
Then knotting them into a rope of love, straight into the sea they went!

'Come back!' cried the lighthouse keeper, 'For God's sake, girls, come back!'
As they caught the waves on their foreheads, resisting the fierce attack.
'Come back!' moaned the grey-haired mother, as she stood by the angry sea,
'If the waves take you my darlings, there's nobody left to me.'
'Come back!' said the three strong soldiers, who still stood faint and pale,
'You will drown if you face the breakers! you will fall if you brave the gale!'
'Come back!' said the girls, 'We will not! go tell it to all the town,

We'll lose our lives, God willing, before that man shall drown!'
'Give one more knot to the shawls, Bess! give one strong clutch of your hand!
Just follow me, brave, to the shingle, and we'll bring him safe to land!
Wait for the next wave, darling! only a minute more,
And I'll have him safe in my arms, dear, and we'll drag him safe to shore.'
Up to the arms in the water, fighting it breast to breast,
They caught and saved a brother alive! God bless us, you know the rest.
Well, many a heart beat stronger, and many a tear was shed,
And many a glass was toss'd right off to 'The Women of Mumbles Head!'

Another act of extreme heroism occurred during that morning, less well-known than that of the Ace sisters. It took place soon after the lifeboat capsized. William Rogers, one of the crew, grasped an oar and passed it to a colleague, Tom Michael. He shouted, 'Here Tom, catch hold of this and then perhaps you will reach the shore.' He was then seen to throw a second oar to another seaman. He bid Tom Michael 'Good Luck', and then said that he was going to attempt to swim out into the bay away from the pounding surf. He was never seen again, and his body was the only one never to be found. Thomas Michael survived the ordeal although he was severely injured. Of the Coxswain's sons, two were drowned and the third had his legs badly crushed.

Ironically, the hull of the *Prinz Adelbert* stayed intact throughout the storm, and at low tide the remaining crew reached the shore safely with the help of the Aces and that of the Artillery men garrisoned at the island fort. The barque even remained intact throughout the next flood tide, but the following day her timbers could be seen floating around the bay. The *Wolverhampton* was found floating, but with her bottom and port side damaged badly. She was towed away by a tug.

At the board of enquiry which followed, the tugs *Flying Scud* and *Flying Cloud* were severely censured for leaving the scene and for not rendering assistance after the arrival of the lifeboat. The *Flying Scud* was especially criticized for breaking her agreement with the Master of the barque, and also for not offering her cables after those on the barque had parted, as would have been normal in such a situation.

A new and slightly larger self-righting lifeboat, also named *Wolverhampton*, was put into service at Mumbles the following month.

Samuel 1884

Outward bound from the Bristol Channel and carrying a cargo of five hundred tons of steam coal, the vessel *Samuel* ran aground on the rocks near Worms Head, Rhossili, one night in 1884. The coastguard and crew were quickly on the scene, and the vessel's crew members brought ashore by Breeches Buoy. The vessel, which was English built, was purchased by a Swansea company, and her cargo of coal was sold to the farmers in the locality. The farmers, in turn, sold the coal to the people of Gower, charging a shilling a cartload, or three pence a bag. The coal was placed in numerous stacks on the grass slopes, each purchaser having his own stack. A road was also cut from the cliff top down to the wreck for easy access to the coal. The remains of this road can still be seen, and is now the footpath which one takes when walking down to Worms Head causeway from the coastguard observation post, which is positioned at the head of the mainland. The coal was a boon to the locals.

The company who bought the vessel was not interested in the profits from the coal, if indeed there were any. It was more interested in the enormous number of copper bolts which secured her hull, and the copper sheathing which protected her timbers. Later, when most of her cargo had been removed, a storm drove her further towards the shore and she began to suffer serious damage. Thoughts of refloating her were now forgotten, and she was finally broken up with explosives; her copper fittings being salvaged. A sale was held to dispose of her spars, sails and other fittings, and Great Pitton farm acquired a large iron fresh-water tank which served its purpose for many years afterwards on dry land. This wreck was not without its tragedy. One of the horses detailed to pull the water tank up the grass slopes fell dead in its harness. Its death was attributed to a heart attack. A rust and barnacle covered anchor from the *Samuel* can still be seen at low water on the causeway.

Ribble and Coniston Fell 1887

On January 26th, 1887, the Mumbles lifeboat *Wolverhampton* was launched in the late evening to assist the steamship *Ribble* of Whitehaven. The *Ribble* had collided with another steamship, the *Coniston Fell* of Liverpool, off Mumbles Head. The *Ribble* was badly damaged and soon began to sink. The lifeboat reached her just as she went down, but fortunately her masts, with her Master and three other men hanging on to them, remained above the surface. Her crew had earlier launched the vessel's boat, but this was lost with two men drowning. One other crew member was picked up by another vessel, and the remaining three managed to cling to the masts along with their captain until saved.

The *Coniston Fell,* although severely damaged, managed to beach herself.

The *Ribble* nearly caused another disaster the following month, when a steam crane barge which had been contracted to lift her, found herself in rough water. The

The 'Helvetia' (National Maritime Museum, Greenwich).

The 'Helvetia' under the sand.

barge had no power of her own, and her Master made a distress signal. The lifeboat was again launched and stood by until the danger had passed.

Helvetia 1887

Of all the wrecks located around the Gower Coast, the most conspicuous and easily examined is that of the *Helvetia* which was lost in 1887 at Rhossili beach. She often pricks the interest of the visitor, and her stout oak timbers serve as a stark memorial to the many vessels which entered this bay never to leave again. On November 1st, 1887, the *Helvetia* and another vessel stood off Mumbles Head flying signals requesting a pilot to board. A South-Easterly gale was blowing at the time, and the pilot cutter was unable to leave the shelter of the bay. As time passed,the gale grew steadily worse and both vessels laden with timber were blown down channel. One of the vessels managed to find shelter at Lundy, but the *Helvetia* struck the notorious Helwick Sandbank. Fortunately, being loaded with timber, she was lifted across the bank, and was blown around the promontory of Worms Head into Rhossili Bay where she found comparatively sheltered water in which to drop anchor. The Rhossili Life Saving Company, led by coastguard Darch, fired a rocket aboard and, although her Master came ashore, he refused completely to leave the scene in case some business-minded person decided to claim his vessel as a prize. Later, when the wind turned to the west, the vessel began to drag her anchor and the crew were all forced to come ashore. When daylight broke, the remains of the *Helvetia* were found on the beach where they can be seen to this day. The vessel had been carrying five hundred tons of wood which was all scattered over the sands, keeping the local villagers, their horses and carts busy for weeks. The cargo was gathered, and auctioned, and many South Wales timber merchants employed ships to remove the wood during the summer. Of all the wrecks in the locality, the *Helvetia* gave the greatest economic boost to the local villagers. Although her crew and Master escaped unhurt, the *Helvetia* was, in later months, to cause tragedy indirectly.

One fine summer's day, two vessels were loading part of the cargo of wood aboard for disposal. One was the steamboat *Cambrian* from Llanelli, and the other was a small sailing vessel from Mumbles. To facilitate an easy departure from the bay, the Master of the sailing vessel carried his anchor to the low water mark, but the *Cambrian,* beginning to float, turned broadside on to the sea.

The Rhossili rocket crew fired a line aboard, and although one man was brought ashore, in the Breeches Buoy, the remainder of the crew remained aboard, there being no great danger to the vessel. On the next tide, her crew followed the example of the Master of the sailing vessel, carrying an anchor to the low water mark. Some time later, the vessel left the bay safely, her anchor remaining stuck firmly in the sand. An anchor which was to bring tragedy.

Several local men were employed to carry the anchor across the sands at low water. They were to leave it attached to a buoy at Kitchen Corner: the idea being that it would be collected at a later date. When the *Cambrian* eventually arrived on a Sunday morning, a boat was lowered and sent to collect the anchor. The boat was manned by six 'landlubbers' out on a day trip. They beached the boat and spent the rest of the day in the Ship Inn. Later in the day, the six men collected the anchor and set out towards the *Cambrian*. For no apparent reason, the small boat capsized spilling her crew into the sea. Five of the six occupants drowned. The only survivor, a fireman, swam ashore.

The *Helvetia*, nevertheless, brought romance, as well as tragedy, to the village of

Rhossili. Her Master and Mate remained in the village for some time after the wrecking of the vessel, probably during the inquest. The Mate was a young Norwegian who fell in love with the eldest of his host's five daughters. A request to marry the girl was refused by her father. No one knows what became of the Norwegian, but the poor girl remained a spinster all her life. She died at the age of eighty.

The Llanelli Pilot Cutters: *Smiling Morn & Maria* 1887

During one night in 1887, the two pilot cutters *Smiling Morn* and *Maria*, both from Llanelli, were anchored under the Inner Head at Rhossili sheltering from a North West gale. The two vessels usually alternated in their duties, one remaining at port, whilst the other took station in Rhossili Bay. Stormy weather became apparent, making it too dangerous to cross the sandbank into Llanelli, so both vessels anchored under the head until the weather improved.

On that particular night, the larger craft, *Smiling Morn*, started to drag her anchor and soon collided with the *Maria*. The force of the collision caused the vessels to hole one another, and soon both began to sink.

The pilots aboard each vessel took to the boats, and managed a hasty, but successful, landing upon Worms Head. Fortunately, they all had a first class knowledge of the coast, otherwise they would all have drowned. The two vessels remained where they had sunk in deep water for many years, until Trinity House eventually decided that the wrecks were becoming a danger to vessels anchoring in

The 'Maria' (National Maritime Museum, Greenwich).

the bay. Their masts were still protruding above the water. A vessel was despatched to destroy the wrecks using explosives.

Not long after the sinking of these two unfortunate vessels, a steam pilot boat came into operation at Llanelli.

Milan 1888

On the evening of January 13th, 1888, the South Gower coast was obscured by a cloak of dense fog. The sea was calm and there was very little wind. Bound from Alexandria for Bristol with her cargo of cotton seed, the Hull steamship *Milan* grounded upon the rocks at Slades Foot, on the cliffs at Overton. The Rhossili Life Saving Apparatus Company, under the command of Coastguard Darch, was quickly on the scene of the incident. The Porteynon lifeboat was launched at 7 p.m., and upon reaching the vessel, took off eleven of the crew. By this time the rescue crew from Rhossili had set up their equipment and successfully fired a line across to the vessel. A hawser was run out and a Breeches Buoy put into operation. The first person to reach the shore by this means was a Mr C. Bevan of Overton. He had gone out to the vessel with the lifeboat to help take off the crew. He explained to the coastguards that the lifeboat had removed several of the *Milan's* crew, and that it would be returning for the remainder. The coastguards, however, decided not to wait for the boat. The remaining seamen were brought ashore by means of the Breeches Buoy.

There was no real danger to the vessel as she had floundered upon a flat bed of rock. Her cargo was removed and she was towed away from the cliff, with little damage to her hull, on the next spring tide.

The 'Ambassador' (National Maritime Museum, Greenwich).

All the *Milan* left behind was her name. It was adopted by the local lifeboat secretary as a fitting name for his new house which he was building at the time, in the village of Overton. It is interesting to note that the *Milan* was the first vessel to need assistance from the Porteynon lifeboat *A Daughter's Offering*.

Ambassador 1890

On January 23rd, 1890, the vessel *Cambrian Duchess,* a large square rigger from Liverpool bound for Iquique in Chile, was pushing up the Bristol Channel in front of a severe gale, after being at sea for a month. She anchored in the Mumbles Roads for shelter, but soon after, her anchors began to drag and she drifted. She collided with the barque *Ambassador* of Aberdeen, losing her own fore and main masts. The *Duchess* was towed by a tug into Swansea, but came to grief yet again when she cast off from the tug too early, and rammed the dock. The Mumbles lifeboat assisted the *Ambassador* to get into Swansea where she was declared a total loss apart from her cargo of coal. The *Cambrian Duchess* sailed again after repairs.

Ashlowe 1890

Three days after the incident involving the *Ambassador* and the *Cambrian Duchess,* another severe gale swept along the Bristol Channel. During the afternoon of January 26th, a coastguard spotted the barque *Ashlowe* of St John, New Brunswick, in distress off Mumbles Head. The Mumbles lifeboat was launched at twenty past four, and it made good speed towards the vessel. The *Ashlowe* had originally been anchored some distance from the shore, but her cable had parted due to her heavy rolling, and she had drifted on to the Green Grounds. The rising tide refloated her, but she drifted in towards the shore at a point near the lifeboat house, finally grounding once more. The heavy seas shook her timbers violently, and to avoid the risk of injury from falling blocks and spars, her Master gave the order to abandon ship. The lifeboat successfully removed the eleven crew members.

Althea 1893

On the night of December 13th, 1893, the Norwegian barque *Althea* grounded on Oxwich beach in a ferocious gale. The Porteynon lifeboat, *A Daughter's Offering*, was launched after great difficulty. On arrival at Oxwich it was found that the vessel was already a total wreck. Near the wreck a light was observed. It was found to be shining from the mast of the vessel's lifeboat. The Porteynon lifeboat closed in towards the small boat, and all the ten crew from the *Althea* were saved.

Glanravil Miner 1894

If one carefully searches in the rocks near Longhole Gut, approximately one mile from Porteynon Head, traces of pitch stains from the *Glanravil Miner* may still be seen. This vessel was driven ashore in heavy seas on March 22nd, 1894. From the shore, observers could plainly see the vessel's crew of three trying desperately to launch the lifeboat. In the conditions that prevailed, it was doubtful if they could reach the shore alive. The Porteynon lifeboat was launched. Upon arrival it was

The 'Verani' at Old Castle Corner, Rhossili.

hailed by a schooner, whose crew told the lifeboat men that they had picked up the stricken vessel's crew soon after they had launched their boat and headed seawards. The three men, along with their effects were transferred to the lifeboat and were safely landed. The vessel quickly broke up, and the sea turned black due to the spillage of her cargo of pitch — the heavy seas causing it to stain the cliff face to this very day.

United Friends 1894

Nine weeks to the day after the loss of the *Glanravil Miner*, the vessel *United Friends* took shelter from a gale in Oxwich Bay. She was on her way to Padstow, in Cornwall, with a consignment of coal. Although she had dropped three anchors, she began to drag towards the white, boiling, surf-filled shore. The Porteynon lifeboat was launched, and the vessel's crew of three, along with their dog, were happily rescued.

Verani 1894

During a period of Easterly winds in 1894, the vessel *Verani*, accompanied by several others, took shelter in Rhossili Bay. One night, whilst the vessels lay at anchor, the wind veered North-West and the *Verani*, which was carrying ballast, began to drag her anchor. Distress rockets were seen coming from her, and the coastguards fired a rocket from the cliff top at Old Castle Point. The vessel, alas, was too far out from the shore, and the rocket fell short of its mark. As the water was at low ebb, the coastguards manhandled their gear down to the sands and prepared for a second attempt to fire a rocket and line aboard. Whilst the rocket equipment was being set up, a light was seen moving from the vessel. The light was lost for a short while, but was then seen again further from the wreck, nearing the shore.

After further observation, a boat was seen outlined against the heavy running seas, and everyone made towards it. The boat beached in the surf and was soon hauled on to dry land by willing hands. The Master of the *Verani* was sitting at the stern of the boat holding a lantern, and next to him sat his wife. The Master congratulated his crew on a job well done, and all were escorted to the village where they were made comfortable.

The Master had used an interesting technique in order to get his boat and crew to the shore in one piece. He had attached a sturdy rope from the stricken vessel to the boat, and paid it out as the boat neared the shore. This allowed the boat to remain head on into the waves, thus surely preventing it from being overturned by the heavy seas. Also, the fact that the boat used was a 'whaler', pointed at both ends, contributed to a successful landing. The following morning, the vessel was to be seen lying in Old Castle Corner, with the rocks tearing at her hull. Her remains can still be seen at low water.

Imbros 1897

In dense fog, on February 2nd, 1897, the Porteynon lifeboat *A Daughter's Offering* was launched to assist a steamer whose whistle could be heard calling from the direction of the Helwick sand bar. The steamer later proved to be the Hull steamship *Imbros,* bound from Constanza with a cargo of barley. The vessel's

The 'Duisberg'.

Master had lost his dead reckoning, and the *Imbros* grounded near the East Helwick Buoy. The heavy seas twisted her hull, opening up gaps in her plates. The life-boat returned to the shore to send for two tugs from Swansea. Then she returned to the stricken vessel. By this time the steamer had managed to get herself off the bank into deeper water where she anchored. Water flooded into her hull, and her damaged engines made her helpless. Fortunately, another steamer in the vicinity took the *Imbros* in tow, with eight feet of water in her hull. The lifeboat stood alongside as far as Oxwich, and the vessel was eventually beached at Mumbles.

Duisberg 1899

During the month of October in 1899 the Norwegian barque *Duisberg* started leaking badly in the middle of the Atlantic. Sixty days earlier she had left Dannoborough in Novia Scotia, carrying a cargo of timber bound for Swansea. The vessel, built in 1857 and of 1026 tons, took in water continuously, and for several weeks her crew slaved at the pumps without rest. The vessel eventually reached the Bristol Channel, but by this time her exhausted crew could no longer manage her. She drifted into Porteynon Bay on November 11th, where she was observed to be behaving in a strange manner. Her behaviour seemed to indicate that she had been abandoned. Although at the time the weather was not stormy, even though the sea was running high. The vessel was first seen by a man and a young boy who were working on the Oxwich Headland. The vessel slowly drifted up the Channel broad-side on, heading towards Oxwich Point. Eventually she turned, and grounded on the rocks at the point, bows on. The young lad was sent hurrying with a message to the coastguard at Oxwich, who in turn, sent a message to the lifeboat crew at Porteynon. The incident was also relayed by telegraph to Swansea, where a Lloyd's

Agent instructed the two tugs *Contest* and *Africa*, to leave immediately for the scene to try to refloat her. The *Africa* was also instructed to take the Mumbles lifeboat in tow.

While the two lifeboats and the tugs were heading towards the *Duisberg*, the latter's crew of fourteen aboard had made their presence known to the spectators on the shore. The crew lowered the vessel's boats, and managed to reach the shore safely at Oxwich Beach. A short while after leaving the barque, her crew watched the vessel's three masts collapse in a tangle of wood, sail and rigging. She soon started to break up under the continuous pounding of the heavy seas, but fortunately, at low tide in the afternoon, she still remained in sufficiently good shape for her crew to re-board to collect their personal effects. Equipment from the vessel was saved with the help of the local villagers. The weather improved over the next few days, enabling her cargo of timber to be salvaged. The timber was stacked on the shore, and a track was made to transport it round to the Eastern side of the headland, where it was made up into rafts and towed away.

Ann of Bridgwater 1899

On December 31st, 1899, a South-West gale blew hard across Rhossili Bay. Distress signals were soon seen from the shore, and a vessel was seen drifting shorewards at a point near Dileslake. The Rhossili Rocket Crew fired a rocket aboard. But strangely enough, there was no sign of her crew. The vessel was not a large one; she was later found to be 120 tons in ballast. Coastguard Reeves boarded as soon as the tide had fallen sufficiently, but the only living thing he saw was the ship's cat. The District Coastguard Officer, Captain Allen from Mumbles, was informed. He took command of the scene upon arrival at the bay. A search of the vessel brought to light the Captain's papers, and by a strange and eerie coincidence, revealed to Captain

Prince of Wales Dock, Swansea, 1900. (Swansea Maritime Museum)

Allen that the vessel's Captain had the same name, and was the same age and height as himself! The vessel was undamaged, so he ordered the rescue crew to carry the anchor to the low water mark. Several volunteers were asked to stay aboard with him to attempt to take the vessel to Llanelli. A coastguard was despatched to Llanelli in order to get a tug to meet the vessel at high water to take her in tow. The volunteers boarded, and at high tide, by using the windlass, managed to move the vessel further from the shore into relatively smooth water. The wind was blowing directly at the shore, thus making it impossible to move the vessel out using her own sails. The crew of volunteers waited for four hours, but the tug never arrived. The tide turned and ebbed, and on New Year's morning, the coastguard and volunteers left her and came ashore. The following night the sea finally won its fight, and broke the vessel to pieces, scattering her timbers all over the bay.

It was later discovered that the crew had been taken off the vessel by the Llanelli Pilot Tug the previous night.

Ethiopia 1900

Bound for Port Talbot from Hamburg, and in ballast, the steamer *Ethiopia* ran aground at Oxwich Point on February 23rd, 1900 because of thick fog. The vessel was first seen on the morning of the 24th. Tugs from Swansea arrived at the scene soon after the Porteynon lifeboat. Vast seas smashed over the vessel, and it appeared as if she would be lost. The lifeboat managed to take stout hawsers, not only to the two tugs, but to a pilot steamer as well. But the *Ethiopia* could not be moved at all. When the tide eventually ebbed, the lifeboat took the steamer's Master to a tug so that he could go to Swansea for further assistance. Some time soon after, the vessel was refloated successfully and taken to a dock at Port Talbot for repairs.

Agot 1900

During November 1900, the barque *Agot* came ashore on Whitford Sands. As there was no rescue company in that vicinity, the one at Rhossili was sent for. Delays in communication and the considerable distance from Rhossili to Whitford, meant that valuable time was lost in reaching the scene. Fortunately, the crew had all been removed from the vessel by a Llanelli Pilot boat. Upon arrival at the vessel, the Rhossili crew found a rather stubborn pilot in charge. He refused to let anyone aboard. Soon afterwards, the vessel's Captain arrived by boat from Llanelli. He smartly ordered the Pilot to remove himself. The Pilot, who had evidently found a locker holding spirits, was in no condition to resist, so he agreed to leave. The deck was a considerable height from the sand, and half-way down the ladder, the Pilot lost his footing and fell into the mud, knocking himself unconscious. The vessel was never saved, and succeeding tides broke her up completely.

S. S. *Evangeline* 1904

At Whitford Sands in 1904 the S.S. *Evangeline* was driven ashore during stormy weather. Although the wind and sea were rough, the vessel being new sustained little damage. Several carts, hired from the locals, used to carry her cargo ashore, almost led to a fight between the crew and the villagers. The incident occurred when a bag of biscuits split open, scattering the contents over the mud. One of the villagers picked up some of the biscuits and placed them in his pocket. Unfortunately, he was observed by one of the crew. The seaman picked up one of the blocks from the ship and threw it at the man. The block missed its target by inches, but severely damaged one of the carts. Fortunately, order was soon restored. During the following months, a channel was cut out of the mud, and the *Evangeline* was refloated in deep water, little the worse for her experience.

Lutece 1909

On December 22nd, 1909, a coastguard observed a steamer aground at Southgate. The vessel was later found to be the French steamship *Lutece,* but when the Porteynon lifeboat *Janet* reached her, the lifeboatmen saw that the vessel had already refloated with the assistance of a tug. The *Lutece* was half full of water and her boilers flooded, but slowly, the tug began to tow her towards Swansea. As the *Lutece* would have had no motive power of her own if she had broken free from the tug, the lifeboat stood alongside for most part of the journey. It is interesting to note that this was the first service of the lifeboat *Janet.*

Leonie 1910

Gower has experienced many bad storms over the years, and on one particular night in 1910, the vessel *Leonie* fell victim to one of them. She was carrying a cargo of pit props at the time, and the pounding seas drove her mercilessly against Tears Point at Fall Bay, smashing her hull. Her Captain, seventy years of age, was badly bruised, but fortunately, no lives were lost. How all survived in such bad weather was hard to comprehend, but Fall Bay soon became a sea of moving wreckage, and for months afterwards, the surrounding nooks and crannies along the coastline were jammed full with pit props. No trace of the wreck was ever found.

The 'S.S. Epidauro' ashore near Overton cliffs.

Epidauro 1913

A thick fog shrouded the south coast of Gower on February 13th, 1913, when a ship's boat, manned by an officer and three crew members of the steamship *Epidauro* came ashore out from the clouds of mist. The officer explained that the ship was Austrian and that she had run aground at the foot of some cliffs which later proved to be at Overton. She had come from the Mediterranean, making for Swansea, carrying ballast. The lifeboat *Janet* was launched at Porteynon to give assistance. One of her crew, who had arrived too late, decided to walk overland to the scene of the wreck. Upon arrival, he found a second ship's boat whose crew had come ashore to join those who had landed earlier. He hurriedly joined them, only to learn that they had all decided to return to the stranded ship. They drew alongside. Three of the crew had safely boarded by means of the ship's ladder, when a huge swell caught the boat and capsized it. The lifeboatman managed to grab a ladder, but the three crew members remaining in the boat were thrown into the sea. Fortunately, the lifeboat had by now arrived and picked up the three men safely. When the tide ebbed, the *Epidauro* was left perched on the rocks and her remaining crew made to the shore safely with the assistance of the Rhossili rescue team, who had been standing by. The vessel became a total wreck a few days later.

Bluebell 1913

At 4 a.m. on February 15th, 1913, distress signals were seen just off Porteynon Point. The lifeboat from Porteynon managed to locate the vessel at Culver Hole, badly holed and full of water. The vessel was the steamship *Bluebell*, and as it

The 'S.S. Bluebell' ashore at Culver Hole near Porteynon.

The ketch 'Leonora' from Padstow, was beached at Langland Bay after being in collision with the tug 'Atlas' on November 19th, 1913. She was put ashore to prevent her from sinking, but became a total loss.

became apparent, later in the day, she was breaking up. The crew of twelve were transferred to the lifeboat and taken ashore. The Captain of the *Bluebell* was an old sea dog from Pembrokeshire. At the enquiry he stated that he had plotted his course from the Helwick light vessel. He had, so he said, instructed his helmsman to steer East by South, but in fact he had steered East by North soon after he himself had gone below. The first he knew of his misfortune, he said, was when the vessel grated on the rocks at Porteynon Point. But by that time it was too late to do anything to save the ship. The steamer broke up quickly, and although her cargo soon washed away, the local villagers managed to salvage sufficient for their immediate needs.

Dunvegan 1916

On January 1st, 1916, the steamship *Dunvegan* from Glasgow came ashore at Oxwich. The vessel lay amid mountainous surf amidst the rocks near the shore, and although the Porteynon lifeboat *Janet* arrived at the scene, the crew were taken off by the rocket company from the shore. This was the last time that the Porteynon boat was to see service, for when making for home in the teeth of the gale, heavy seas struck the lifeboat causing it to overturn twice, spilling nearly all her crew overboard. Most of these men managed to grab the life lines and board again. When a roll call was made, it was discovered that William Gibbs the Coxswain, Second Coxswain William Eynon, and a lifeboatman George Harry were missing.

The remaining crew turned the boat around with the oars and began a search. It was thought possible that the three men could have stayed afloat in their lifejackets for a short while. But the three men were drowned. The bodies of Eynon and Harry were later recovered. They are now interred in the churchyard at Porteynon. George

TO
THE GLORY OF GOD
AND IN MEMORY OF
WILLIAM (BILLY) GIBBS, COXSWAIN
WILLIAM EYNON, SECOND COXSWAIN
GEORGE HARRY, LIFEBOATMAN
WHO WERE DROWNED OFF PWLL-DU
ON 1ST JANUARY 1916 WHEN THE PORTEYNON
LIFEBOAT "JANET" TWICE CAPSIZED IN THE
ENDEAVOUR TO RENDER ASSISTANCE
TO THE S.S. "DUNVEGAN"

THE SURVIVING MEMBERS OF THE CREW
CAPTN. GEO. EYNON, WM. GROVE, SEN.
WM. GROVE, JNR, ONSLOW GROVE
WM. HARRIS, WM. HOWELL,
JOHN JENKINS, CHAS JENKINS,
LEONARD JENKINS, JOHN MORRIS,
AFTER GREAT SUFFERING SUCCEEDED IN
LANDING AT MUMBLES THE FOLLOWING MORNING

THE BODIES OF WM. EYNON AND GEO. HARRY
WERE EVENTUALLY RECOVERED AND ARE
INTERRED IN THIS CHURCH YARD

ERECTED BY VOLUNTARY SUBSCRIPTIONS TO
COMMEMORATE BRAVERY AND
DEVOTION TO DUTY.

The memorial to the lifeboat 'Janet' at Porteynon Church.

Eynon took command of the boat, and realizing the impossibility of reaching Porteynon along to the West, he decided to make for Mumbles. They arrived there the following day after twenty four hours at sea, each man badly shaken and suffering from exposure.

After this tragedy and ordeal the lifeboat was never replaced at Porteynon. The station was abandoned. A memorial at the village church in Porteynon stands in tribute to those who lost their lives on that inhuman day.

Tridonia 1916

Seventeen years after the loss of the *Duisberg* at Oxwich, and almost at exactly the same point, the Gower Coast claimed its biggest victim. The vessel was the *Tridonia,* a sailing ship, which when built, was the French barque *Jean Bart.* Later in her career, she was sold by the French to the Germans and was re-christened *Heinz.* On August 4th, 1914, however, when the First World War was declared, she found herself being loaded with her first cargo in a British port. The vessel was immediately interned and later re-fitted and re-named. Her first voyage in the hands of the British was to collect a cargo of grain from the River Plate. She was under the command of Captain Stewart from Aberdeen, and in October 1916 sailed from Dublin. The Captain's wife was also aboard. The vessel met very rough weather in the Atlantic, and after losing a set of sails, it turned back and put into Cork. Several days later, the weather moderated and for the second time the *Tridonia* left the shores of Ireland on her voyage across the Atlantic. She again ran into rough weather, again losing her sails. With the masts stripped of canvas, she was pushed up the Bristol Channel by the force of the gale. On Sunday October 29th, she

The 'Tridonia'.

The 'Beaufort'

anchored in Porteynon Bay to avoid grounding on the many sand banks.

Captain Stewart signalled for a pilot and was met by the cutter *Beaufort.* Four attempts were then made in the surging seas before a Swansea pilot, Captain W. J. Davies, was finally put aboard. The gale force winds and the rolling waters put a tremendous strain on the cables of the *Tridonia,* and upon Captain Davies's advice, springs were fitted to absorb the shock. The vessel sat in the bay intent on riding out the storm, but at 10 a.m. on the following morning, the wind rose to hurricane force and one by one her cables parted. She quickly drove hard against the rocks bows on, and soon she began to settle, swamped from bow to stern by heavy seas.

Volunteers were called in by Captain Stewart in order to attempt to get a line ashore. The ship's boat was lowered and the First Mate, the carpenter and two other crew members set off towards the shore. The small boat had hardly moved forward at all, before it was swamped by the heavy seas. Fortunately, the four men managed to reach the shore safely. The remaining crew and Mrs Stewart were ordered forward as the cabin was now beginning to break up. The masts were now in danger of collapse, and canvas shelters were rigged up on the jib-boom and Mrs Stewart was lashed to the bowspit.

The Oxwich rocket crew fired all their rockets in an attempt to get a line aboard the vessel, but the wind proved to be too strong. Later in the evening at approximately eight o'clock, the Rhossili Rocket Crew arrived. With the tide now ebbing, the rocket apparatus was set up on the now exposed rocks. Two rockets were fired but these both failed to reach their target. A third rocket was fired and this, it was found, had caught on to something, although on what, it was too dark to tell. When daylight came, all ashore were amazed to see the vessel's masts still standing. The crew, no longer fearing their collapse, had moved to the relative safety of the masts. More important, however, it could be seen that the rocket which had been fired in the night, was across the ship, and when the rescue crew hauled it up out of the water, the ship's crew saw it and secured it fast. Soon after, the Breeches Buoy was sent out to the vessel and the rescue operation started. Mrs Stewart was the first person to be brought ashore. She immediately asked if anyone had been found during the night, explaining that her husband and one of the crew had been washed overboard in the night. But they were never found alive. In fact, the Captain's body was found at Aberavon Beach several days later. Approximately a hundred people had now gathered at the scene, and with everyone helping to haul ashore, the remaining crew, some twenty men in all, were quickly brought to dry land. Soon after daylight the Tenby lifeboat appeared about a mile off shore, but it could not get in closer. The Mumbles boat, which had also been launched, had to turn back at Oxwich Point due to the heavy seas.

It is interesting to note two incidents which occurred on that night of the disaster. The first involved a young boy from Rhossili who, seeing that the weather whip (which forms part of the rescue line to the vessel) had caught on some rocks, climbed inside the bight and, upon clearing the obstruction, he was thrown back and hurled unconscious against the rocks. Fortunately, he recovered, and in later years he became a member of the Rhossili Rescue Company. The second incident occurred when the crew were being hauled ashore. Several young boys, who had been watching the drama, noticed some black objects in the water a little further up the coast. Upon investigation, the objects were found out to be three black pigs which the crew of the *Tridonia* had thrown overboard. The animals were safely brought ashore, but had to be placed in quarantine for several months. The vessel's crew, who were in bad shape, were taken care of by the villagers for several days afterwards. Mrs Stewart recovered sufficiently to be moved to Swansea the following day. The *Tridonia* became a total wreck without ever having carried a cargo. At the time

The schooner 'Fleur de France' aground on the Mixons

The 'S.S. Tyne' aground at Langland Bay

The Swansea pilot cutter 'Beaufort', did much to assist vessels in distress during the years prior to the establishment of an official lifeboat at Mumbles.

that she was lost, she was one of the few survivors of the days of sail. The Gower coast was to claim many more vessels, but the *Tridonia* was the last vessel of her type to be lost in Gower waters.

Tyne 1919

On April 19th, 1919, bound for London and sailing via Swansea, the Royal Mail Lines steamer *Tyne* collided with the *Fleur de Mer,* a French schooner outward bound from Cardiff, in heavy fog. The latter vessel was cut into two, but her crew manned their small boat which they always towed behind. The *Tyne* eventually helped the schooner's crew to safety, but in her search for them lost her bearings and ran on to the shore at Langland Bay. The sea and wind at the time were calm, and the fifty-odd men aboard managed to reach dry land safely by wading ashore. Although the vessel was reported to have broken her back, she was refloated and towed back into Swansea ten days later.

Fleur de France 1920

On April 1st, 1920, the vessel *Fleur de France* grounded on the Mixon sand bar. Her crew managed to abandon her safely in their small boat, and all were later picked up by the *Beaufort,* a pilot cutter. Coastguards had observed the incident from the shore. A little after midnight on the morning of the 2nd, the Mumbles lifeboat *Charlie Medland* was launched to give assistance. Eventually, the lifeboat met the *Beaufort* and after her crew had exchanged a few words with that of the cutter, they decided to try and save the schooner.

The French schooner 'Raven' driven ashore in 1923

Several lifeboatmen were put aboard along with some of the schooner's crew. They later managed to refloat her on the flood tide. A tow rope was attached, and the *Beaufort* managed to beach the vessel at Mumbles. She was very badly damaged, but was eventually taken away for repairs.

Raven 1923

October 27th, 1923, saw the French schooner *Raven* being driven against the shore in Swansea Bay before a severe South South-West gale. The lifeboat *Charlie Medland* was launched from Mumbles. It experienced great difficulty in removing the crew from the stricken vessel. The *Raven* became totally wrecked and the gale rose to such force that the lifeboat itself was driven before the wind towards the town. She later returned to Mumbles with the assistance of a tug. This rescue, incidentally, was the last service of the *Charlie Medland* before she was replaced by the new *Edward Prince of Wales*.

Ben Blanche 1933

One night in 1933, thick fog drifted around the Gower cliffs when the *Ben Blanche*, bound for Swansea and carrying potatoes, grounded at Paviland. The Rhossili Rocket Crew were alerted and they soon set up their equipment. A rocket line was fired across to the vessel, but the rescue crew observed no life whatsoever. Mystified and concerned, they awaited the dawn when they learnt that the whole crew had left the vessel in their own boat. The sea was calm at the time, and the crew

The 'Roche Castle'.

had been picked up safely in the channel by another vessel. The *Ben Blanche* soon afterwards became a total wreck, and her remains were later cut up and sold as scrap. This wreck, incidentally, caused the collapse of an excellent lobster hole which had been fished for many years by the locals.

Roche Castle 1937

The Swansea trawler *Roche Castle* returning home on a dark, rough and foggy night in 1937, ran ashore at Paviland Cliff. The Rhossili Rescue Company was alerted and a rocket was successfully fired aboard at the first attempt, the vessel being steady. The Breeches Buoy was run out and made fast to the mast, but the vessel's Captain, thinking that he could refloat her on the flood tide, refused to come ashore. As the tide rose, the vessel lurched and began to roll over the rocks.

This motion caused the rescue line and hawser to slacken off and submerge in the water. The cables then strained to such an extent that it was feared they would snap. The crew began to panic and the Captain gave the order to abandon the vessel. As the first crew member left the vessel in the Breeches Buoy, another seaman, who was stricken with panic, leapt into the Buoy but was washed away and drowned. Great difficulty was experienced performing the rescue due to the ship's continuous motion. Happily though, all the remaining crew were brought ashore safely.

This particular rescue was held in high esteem by the Board of Trade, and resulted in the rescue company being awarded the Board's shield for the best executed rescue of the year. The shield was greatly honoured, and doubly so due to the fact that it was the first time for it to be awarded to a Welsh company.

Eldon Park 1940

On the morning of February 7th, 1940, the Mumbles lifeboat *Edward Prince of Wales* was launched in order to assist the steamship *Eldon Park* of Greenock, which reportedly was grounded at Port Eynon. Arriving at the scene, the lifeboat found that the vessel had already sunk, and only the wheelhouse was still visible with the whole crew of thirty seven seeking shelter in it. All the men were taken off safely, but the steamer was a total loss.

Cornish Rose 1941

A South-East gale blew hard across Swansea Bay on the morning of January 21st, 1941. Just after seven o'clock a distress rocket was seen. Rolling heavily, the *Cornish Rose* of Liverpool dragged her anchors towards the rocky shore. The Mumbles lifeboat was launched, and guided only by a small lamp aboard the stricken vessel, managed to ger herself alongside. The lifeboat was battered heavily by the raging seas, her cockpit frequently being flooded. She was in great danger herself from being dragged onto the steel rails which had been positioned in the sand as coastline defences, but miraculously she managed to avoid them. With extreme difficulty, the crew of the *Cornish Rose* succeeded in transferring safely to the lifeboat and in a short while they were safely ashore at Mumbles. For performing this dangerous rescue, the lifeboat Coxswain, William Gammon, and the Mechanic, Robert Williams, were each awarded the R.N.L.I. bronze medal.

The Mumbles lifeboat 'William Gammon', named after the Coxswain who was lost with his entire crew in 1947 when their lifeboat 'Edward Prince of Wales' was smashed against the rocks at Sker Point, near Porthcawl, whilst endeavouring to assist the steamship 'Samtampa'.

Royal Naval Destroyer 'H.M.S. 'Cleveland', 1957.

Solar 1945

Visitors to Oxwich are able to see the scant remains of the Norwegian tanker *Solar* positioned just off the eastern side of the head. The *Solar* was torpedoed in Cardigan Bay in January 1945, and although she was sinking, she was taken in tow and finally beached at Oxwich. She was carrying seven and a half thousand tons of oil, and thirty seven crates of aeroplane parts, all of which were salvaged. The *Solar* lay in the bay for many years afterwards and became a familiar land and sea mark before it was decided to break her up for scrap. Incidentally, this event was one of the last U-boat successes of the last war.

Cleveland 1957

In June 1957, Her Majesty's Ship *Cleveland* ran aground at Llangennith Beach. She had lost her tow line when she was being towed down the Bristol Channel from Cardiff to her final berth at the Llanelli breaker's yard. The *Cleveland* had been designed and built as a fighting ship, and she had decided not to give herself up so easily to the blow torches and hammers at this late stage of her career.

She had picked her spot well, high up on the water line on the beach parallel with the sand dunes with her bows pointing towards Burry Holm. The same week, the salvage crews tried to refloat her, but the *Cleveland* stood her ground defying the powerful tugs and heavy winches. She became a well known toursit attraction, and hoards of visitors from miles around came to 'have a look'. Among visitors were members of her wartime crew who came to reminisce and to pay their last respects.

Several such unsuccessful attempts were made in the weeks following. In the

The 'Cleveland' (National Maritime Museum, Greenwich).

succeeding November, a major attempt was made to refloat her when the tides were at their highest. Storm clouds gathered on the night of the big pull. The *Cleveland* had a friend in the sea itself. The high tides provided sufficient water to refloat her, but the weather made the conditions far too rough. As the tide reached the highest point, the tug boats were safe and snug in the safety of the Port of Swansea. Huge seas battered against the hull of the *Cleveland,* causing the vessel to lurch violently, then, in the words of the salvage crew's specialist officer, Captain R. Scarr, 'The great grandfather of all waves' slammed against the ship, causing the winch cable to snap, and causing the hauling gear to go overboard. It was a moment of triumph for the *Cleveland,* on the eighty eighth day since she had sought refuge at Llangennith. Captain Scarr's decision to remove the seven-man party off the ship for safety, crowned the triumph.

It took nearly two years before the salvage crews admitted they were all beaten, and it was obvious that she did not intend to go to sea again. The *Cleveland* was not to be allowed to join the several other wrecks on the beach to rot. The British Iron and Steel Federation was allocated a contract to break her up where she so defiantly stood. The Federation gave the assurance that the beach would look as good as new on completeion of the job. Another problem made itself evident almost at once. There was no access to the beach for the necessary heavy equipment to be transported to the site; so a somewhat primitive roadway, which still exists, was cut through the dunes. Hundreds of sleepers were laid along this road to support the heavy cranes and lorries, and very soon the glare of the oxy-acetylene burners could be seen. Gradually, the *Cleveland* began to lose her familiar profile, but the old warrior was not beaten yet. She threw a new challenge to the feet of the men who came to destroy her. The aft end of the ship had been cut away level with the beach, but there were still several feet of the hull below. Each successive tide filled her hull

The 'Cleveland' stranded at Llangennith beach.

with sand and water, and the task of breaking up her remaining structure became a tale of despair. High explosives were brought in to carry on from where conventional cutting methods had failed. On 14th December, 1959, the engineer in charge of the breaking operations told the *Evening Post* reporters, 'When we have cleared up the beach after today's explosion, there will be nothing, absolutely nothing, left here of the *Cleveland.*' The final explosion had been planned for 3 p.m. the previous day, but word had got around, and when the time came, it was decided that it was unsafe to explode a major charge with so many onlookers in the vicinity. But, the remaining piece of the destroyer *Cleveland* was blown out of the beach by a charge comprising a hundred sticks of dynamite. In all, seven thousand sticks of dynamite had been used, and three thousand cylinders of oxygen. The following week, Admiralty bulldozers operated over a wide area of beach to ensure that no trace of the vessel remained on or under the surface of the sand. Thus it was, that the ship which had been designed to fight, and which reminded everyone that she still knew how, vanished for ever from the sand and mud which had been her proud home for two and a half years.

The *Cleveland* belonged to the Navy's Hunt class, and was built in Glasgow and launched in 1940. Three months after launching, she was attached to the 1st Destroyer Flotilla based at Portsmouth. She escorted convoys for several months into and from the Thames Estuary and into the English Channel, and was frequently under enemy air attack. In December 1941, she was transferred to the 15th Destroyer Flotilla, Plymouth Command. Her main armament consisted of four four-inch guns, and two twenty millimetre anti-aircraft guns. She was capable of a maximum speed of nearly thirty knots, and assumed her first attacking rôle in March 1942. She gave support for the Combined Operation Force which swooped on enemy positions at St Nazaire under the code name 'Chariot', the raid being successfully carried out by Commandos. During the latter months of 1942, *Cleveland* was on Atlantic escort duties. Then in October she was engaged in the North African landings.

In March 1945, *Cleveland* operated almost daily in support of land forces attacking the Franco-Italian border. Her last major action was the bombardment of Genoa, when she fired 126 shells in the attack. After eleven years in mothballs, *Cleveland* was approved for scrap, but as we have seen, not without a fight.

Kilo 1963

Although one cannot refer to the *Kilo* as a wreck in the accepted sense of the word, the incident involving her which took place on November 18th, 1963 is worth mentioning. The *Kilo* of Amsterdam, was bound for Rotterdam from Liverpool carrying an assorted cargo of cylinders of compressed gas, machine tools, barrels of grease, whisky, cotton and a deck cargo of drums of Sodium. When passing the entrance to the Bristol Channel and approximately thirty five miles south of the Smalls lighthouse, fire broke out on deck. The fire became serious, and the drums of Sodium, upon reaching their flash-point, exploded, scattering the vessel with their blazing contents. The crew tried to fight the fire with water hoses, but being Sodium, the chemical could not be easily extinguished by water. Burning masses of Sodium were pushed overboard, but the fire still held its grip. The *Kilo* radioed her predicament at approximately 7 p.m. on November 17th, and headed for Swansea. Nothing further was heard from her, and it was feared that she was in serious trouble. A general alert was broadcast over the air asking local shipping to keep a look-out and to report if they saw anything. A Shackelton aircraft was sent from its

Swansea firemen aboard the 'Kilo' at South Dock.

RAF base at St Mawgan in Cornwall, and at approximately 10p.m. the Padstow lifeboat was launched. At midnight, the *Kilo* reported again and gave her position as fourteen miles north of Lundy. This information, coupled with the fact that the sea conditions were very bad, resulted in the Padstow lifeboat being recalled, as it would have been impossible for her to catch up with the burning vessel. The Tenby lifeboat was launched, but found the going hard in waves of twenty five feet in height. In fact, it was damaged by these waves — one carrying away a wheelhouse door and smashing another. The *Kilo* reported that the Sodium drums were still exploding, and at 1 a.m. on the morning of the 18th she reported that she had suffered a major explosion, and that she required immediate assistance.

At this point, she was ten miles east of the Helwick light vessel, the crew of which, on seeing the explosion, radioed the position of the *Kilo*. The Tenby lifeboat and the vessels *Oreasa, Porjus* and *Chailey* approached to give what assistance they could. The Shackelton, on finding the *Kilo*, illuminated the scene with parachute flares. The vessel was now close to Swansea, and the Mumbles lifeboat, launched at 3.30 a.m., battled towards the vessel through the twenty foot waves. The lifeboatmen sighted the *Kilo* in the eerie lights of the flares, and the vessel appeared to be a mass of flames with the surrounding sea ablaze with burning Sodium. The Coxswain positioned the boat as near as possible, and he ordered several of his crew forward to help the crew of the *Kilo* come aboard. The burning Sodium falling off the ship proved to be too much of a hazard, so that the lifeboatmen had to hurry back to the safety of the boat's cockpit. The Coxswain decided to make a run-in towards the vessel, but a massive wave smashed over the boat and the attempt was aborted. On the second run-in, the ship suddenly lurched, as a massive sea crashed over her decks. At almost the same instant, there was a large explosion with flames shooting high in the air. But the lifeboatmen managed to avoid a collision. A third attempt was prepared to approach close to the ship, when suddenly the flames died down.

Captain Hoogenveen, the Master of the *Kilo,* hailed the lifeboat to say that he would not abandon his vessel, but would try to beach her at Mumbles. This he managed to do successfully thirty minutes later, with the lifeboat and the Swansea pilot cutter *Seamark* equipped with fire pumps, standing by. The pumps were not used, as it was realized that the addition of water to the burning Sodium would only make matters worse. The fire in the holds spread, and fearing that a major explosion in the hold might tear the ship apart, Captain Hoogenveen finally decided to abandon ship. The lifeboat finally came in close to the stern, and the ten crew members were safely taken off the burning vessel.

Several hours later and whilst still burning, the *Kilo* refloated on the flood tide. The risk of explosion was still too great for a crew to board her, but eventually the fire died down and the *Seamark* managed to attach a tow line. When it was considered that the risk of explosion had diminished, the lifeboat returned the Captain and Engineer to the vessel. Finding that her engines could be restarted, the vessel docked under her own power, battered, but still afloat.

THE SECOND WORLD WAR SHIPPING CASUALTIES — and some more recent ones.

Marwarri 1939

The coming of the second world war posed a new threat to shipping visiting our shores, that of the mining of our coastal regions by the Germans. Many tons of shipping were lost as a result of this action, and vessels entering the Bristol Channel by no means escaped the ever-present danger the mines imposed.

One of the first vessels ever to come into contact with the then new 'magnetic mines' was the 7,800 ton *S/S Marwarri*. She was mined in the Bristol Channel on September 12, 1939 but managed to reach the Mumbles where she was beached. Damage to her was not serious and she was eventually towed away for repairs.

Lochgoil 1939

Another victim of the German mines was the 8,534 ton Royal Mail ship *Lochgoil*. She was bound for Vancouver from Newport when she struck a mine whilst at a position approximately five miles from the Scarweather lightship on October 6th, 1939. The vessel eventually sank, but fortunately for the 45 persons aboard, a Cardiff vessel which was in the immediate vicinity came to the rescue and took everyone off. The reserve lifeboat from Mumbles *J. B. Proudfoot* was launched in order to assist, and escorted the Cardiff vessel back to Mumbles where she landed all 45 persons ashore.

This service, incidentally, was the first war service launch from the Mumbles station.

Floating crane which broke adrift being pulled by the tug 'Cardiff' at Kenfig Sands.

Breeches Buoy in action.

Nora 1940's

The photograph below shows the remains of the Dutch vessel *Nora,* which sank near the shore after striking a German mine. Another mine can be seen to the left of the picture. This was later destroyed.

Witte Zee 1940

During the winter months of 1940, there occurred an exciting drama at Overton Mere near Porteynon when the 211 ton Dutch trawler *Witte Zee* drove ashore. The vessel had fallen foul of a severe gale whilst off the west coast, and the raging winds had pushed her into the Bristol Channel.

Her Master fired several distress rockets, and then left the vessel in a small boat with two of his crew in an effort to summon help. The gale was still blowing hard though, and the heavy seas soon swamped the boat, smashing it against the rocks and spilling its three occupants into the raging surf.

Two Coastguards at Porteynon had seen the distress flares and hurried to the scene. They soon observed the three men struggling in the sea, and disregarding the danger to themselves, both of them waded into the waves and pulled one of the men ashore to safety.

A police constable by the name of Mabbett, who had been telephoned for help, arrived at the scene, and wading out into the water he succeeded in dragging another of the men to safety.

Coastguard Dodd in the meantime had observed other crew members jump from the stricken vessel. He immediately started swimming towards the ship, and eventually managed to save the Captain and two other seamen. The remaining crew stayed aboard and were eventually brought ashore by means of rocket line.

All the crew, a total of eighteen including the Master, were brought ashore without loss of life, and the fact that all of them were from a friendly country seemed to make the efforts of the two Coastguards and Constable Mabbett seem that much more worthwhile.

Protelisaus 1940

On the very damp morning of January 21st, 1940, Mumbles Coastguards reported that a vessel which was thought to have been mined was sinking off Mumbles Head. The sinking vessel turned out to be the 9,577 ton *Protelisaus* of Liverpool. The Mumbles lifeboat was launched, but arriving at the scene found a naval vessel standing-by taking off the crew and passengers. The naval vessel had up to that point taken off fifty three persons, but the lifeboat removed the remainder. The *Protelisaus* was owned by the Blue Funnel Company, and was their first-ever casualty.

A number of weeks after this incident she was towed into Mumbles and beached at West Cross where she eventually broke her back.

St Kearan 1949

On October 12th, 1949 the steam coaster *St Kearan* was bound from Cardiff in order to pick up a cargo of coal. During the voyage, however, the vessel started to leak seriously and although her crew attempted to stem the flow of water using pumps, the situation became uncontrolable. Her Master fearing the loss of the vessel, drove her ashore on the beach at Oystermouth. Her beaching caused slight damage to her hull, but temporary repairs were made and eventually she was towed into Swansea docks for further repairs and examination.

The *St Kearan*, 394 tons, was built in 1921 and registered at Glasgow.

The 'Riverton' at King's Dock, Swansea after her repairs to damage sustained from grounding at Nash Sands.

Riverton 1945

A familiar sight off Mumbles Head during the post war years was the remains of the stern of the 4,179 ton *Riverton*. She had been torpedoed off Lands End in 1945, and with her stern almost blown away, she was towed into Swansea. She was taken into the Prince of Wales dry dock where her stern was temporarily repaired and later went on to the Tyne where a brand new stern was fitted.

Her original stern remained at Mumbles and became such a well known feature of the bay, that tourists were often ferried out to her 'to have a look' by enterprising local boatmen until she was later blown up by the authorities.

The *Riverton* made a return visit to Swansea docks in 1949, when she underwent minor repairs after grounding off Nash Sands.

Barry Castle 1949

On August 23rd, 1949 the 300 ton steam trawler *Barry Castle* berthed at Swansea South Dock in order to load on sixty tons of ice for her return trip to the Icelandic fishing grounds. Loading was commenced and continued into the night, but at about 11.45 p.m. the vessel began to turn over at her moorings, and by just after midnight she was well over on to her port side. Her stern became completely submerged but fortunately none of her crew were aboard at the time. Efforts were made to prevent any further movement, and eventually the vessel was righted.

The *Barry Castle* had been built in 1942 and was owned by Consolidated Fisheries Ltd., and had a Swansea registration. She was the first ever Swansea trawler to venture into Icelandic waters, and had been fitted out for this rôle in Grimsby as part

The 'Barry Castle' which sank at South Dock, Swansea.

The 'Atlantic Duchess' 1951.

of an experiment brought about by poor results from fishing in local waters.

She had returned from her first fishing expedition on June 8th after twenty two days at sea, and although the weather throughout the trip had been attrocious, her catch was considered good enough to allow the continuation of the experiment.

Atlantic Duchess 1951

The early hours of February 2nd, 1951 proved to be a black mark in the history of the Port of Swansea, for this was the night when a Liberian registered tanker *Atlantic Duchess* was wrecked by a series of explosions followed by fire while berthed at Queen's Dock.

The *Atlantic Duchess* arrived at Swansea two days earlier with a cargo of 12,000 tons of oil from Abadan. She had been discharged of her cargo and all pipe lines disconnected when two violent explosions broke her back. The explosions sent flames 35 feet into the air, and were of such force that townsfolk within a radius of five miles were awakened from their sleep.

Most of the Greek crew were aboard at the time, and all had a rude awakening as they were thrown from their bunks. Captain Kaminis Bodkis picked himself up from the floor of his cabin only to find himself surrounded by flames. He later stated that had the wind been from any other direction, he probably would not have escaped with his life.

Eye witnesses within the dock area summoned the Swansea fire brigade, but such was the seriousness of the situation that both the Neath and Pontardawe services were called in for support. A third major explosion rocked the vessel at 10.45 in the morning, injuring six firemen, two of whom were thrown into the dock. The fire was eventually brought under control, but the danger of further explosions existed for many days afterwards due to residual oil and gas pockets. The disaster had left the vessel with a 35° list, a broken back, and with her bridge and superstructure completely destroyed.

The explosions had killed seven of her forty-man crew, several bodies not being recovered until several days later.

The vessel had celebrated her maiden voyage only a few months earlier when she had left her builders in Hartlepool to voyage to the Persian Gulf. Her visit to Swansea was the first time she had returned to British waters since launching. The residual oil and gas were eventually removed, and marine engineers upon examining her condition decided that she was in fact salvageable. On March 21st her bow section was towed out of Swansea and returned to Hartlepool. Her stern half followed in April, both halves to be eventually rebuilt.

Steam Fisher 1952

Another vessel which met with disaster within the confines of the dock area at Swansea was the 746 ton motor vessel *Steam Fisher*. She had arrived from Holland on August 31st with nearly a thousand tons of pig iron aboard which was duly discharged. Her next voyage was to have been to France with a cargo of 800 tons of Anthracite coal, and loading was commenced the same day at King's Dock. The following morning as loading continued and the vessel began to settle deeper, water started pouring into her engine room through open portholes.

Work was stopped on the vessel immediately, and efforts were made to stem the flow of water. Firemen did the best they could, and the Britannia Towing Company's tug *Clyneforth* which was equipped with pumps for fire fighting, was

The 'Martaban' at Swansea during one of her visits to the port.

called in in an attempt to pump the water from the vessel. All efforts proved fruitless and the *Steam Fisher*'s crew were obliged to leave. The *Clyneforth* positioned herself in an attempt to keep the sinking vessel's stern level, but was ordered to stand clear while further coal was loaded in order to regain the *Steam Fisher's* balance. The battle was eventually lost, and the stricken vessel began to roll over, two of her crew just managing to escape in time and board the tug.

The *Clyneforth* tried to wedge the vessel against the dock to prevent her sinking, but had to manoeuvre clear quickly to avoid serious damage as the *Steam Fisher* capsized and sank to the dock floor.

Several days later, operations were commenced to salvage the coal, and by early the following month most of it was recovered with the assistance of a floating crane and a team of hard-working divers. The *Steam Fisher* herself was raised several weeks later.

She had been built at Sunderland in 1943 and was originally named the *Empire Judy*. She was registered at Barrow and owned by Messrs James Fisher and Co. Ltd.

Martaban 1952

On September 11th, 1952 the *Martaban*, a 5,740 ton cargo vessel caught fire whilst on passage from Avonmouth to Liverpool with a cargo of cotton seed, baled cotton, bran, rice and ground nut oil cake. She had been built in 1950 by William Denny and Brothers Ltd for the British and Burmese Steam Navigation Co. Ltd, and had originally started her voyage from Rangoon, only berthing at Avonmouth to off-load part of her cargo.

On her way to Liverpool, the Officer on watch discovered the fire at 3 a.m. and the vessel set course for Swansea, the Mumbles Coastguard being contacted by signal lamp. The Mumbles lifeboat was launched at 5.30 a.m. and stood by the burning ship as a precaution.

At Swansea docks, the tug *Clyneforth* which was equipped with fire fighting apparatus, put out from port, and the pilot cutter *Seamark* with portable pumps aboard also made for the burning vessel. Although no one aboard the *Martaban* had so far been injured, the nature of her cargo was causing considerable concern. The oil content of the cotton seed was a particular risk, and the fact that wet grain swells when heated did nothing to ease the situation.

The pilot cutter *Seamark* put alongside the *Martaban* at approximately 6.30 a.m., but upon returning later to leave the firemen and their equipment aboard, found that the fire had established a firm grip in No. 4 hold. The *Martaban*'s deck and side plates were observed to be shedding their paint under the intense heat, and the crew aboard the pilot cutter could feel the heat radiating against their skins from the burning hold.

As dawn spread across the bay, the *Martaban* was being towed towards the dock by the tugs *Clyneforth, Waterloo* and *Brockenhurst*. The stricken vessel finally berthed at King's Dock at 10.50 a.m. and firemen immediately put aboard more powerful pumps. Assistance was also given by the British Petroleum fire float *BP Firemaster* from Queen's Dock.

Within forty minutes of berthing, water was being pumped into the *Martaban*'s holds at a rate of 1,500 gallons per minute, causing great clouds of smoke and steam to belch out and cover the entire dock area. The fire was also kept in check by steam injection, and eventually after a hard and dirty fight, the firemen managed to beat the flames. Thousands of gallons of water had been pumped into her holds, and as a result the stricken *Martaban* had developed a bad list to starboard whilst berthed at the dock wall. She was eventually righted and later completely repaired.

First launch of the new Mumbles lifeboat, the 'Pentland', August 1974. (Evening Post).